COLLEGE SUCCESS
FOR STUDENTS WITH
LEARNING
DISABILITIES

STRATEGIES AND TIPS TO MAKE THE MOST OF YOUR COLLEGE EXPERIENCE

COLLEGE SUCCESS
FOR STUDENTS WITH
LEARNING DISABILITIES

CYNTHIA G. SIMPSON, PH.D., AND VICKY G. SPENCER, PH.D.

PRUFROCK PRESS INC.
WACO, TEXAS

Library of Congress Cataloging-in-Publication Data

Simpson, Cynthia G.
  College success for students with learning disabilities / Cynthia G. Simpson & Vicky G. Spencer.
    p. cm.
  Includes bibliographical references.
  ISBN-13: 978-1-59363-359-2 (pbk.)
  ISBN-10: 1-59363-359-9 (pbk.)
  1. Learning disabled—Education (Higher)—United States—Handbooks, manuals, etc. 2. College student orientation—United States—Handbooks, manuals, etc. I. Spencer, Vicky G. II. Title.
  LC4818.38.S56 2009
  371.91—dc22
                          2009002591

Copyright © 2009 Prufrock Press Inc.
Edited by Lacy Compton
Cover and Layout Design by Marjorie Parker

ISBN-13: 978-1-59363-359-2
ISBN-10: 1-59363-359-9

Printed in the United States of America.

At the time of this book's publication, all facts and figures cited are the most current available. All telephone numbers, addresses, and Web site URLs are accurate and active. All publications, organizations, Web sites, and other resources exist as described in the book, and all have been verified. The authors and Prufrock Press Inc. make no warranty or guarantee concerning the information and materials given out by organizations or content found at Web sites, and we are not responsible for any changes that occur after this book's publication. If you find an error, please contact Prufrock Press Inc.

Prufrock Press Inc.
P.O. Box 8813
Waco, TX 76714-8813
Phone: (800) 998-2208
Fax: (800) 240-0333
http://www.prufrock.com

We would like to dedicate this book to those individuals with disabilities who have chosen to follow the college dream and to those individuals who may not have realized that college was a possibility. May you find yourselves examining this opportunity and reaching your full academic potential.

We also would like to dedicate this book to our families. Our husbands and children have provided us with love, support, and continued words of encouragement. We could not have done it without you. Thank you!

CONTENTS

ACKNOWLEDGEMENTS

There are many people who have contributed to the process of writing this book. First and foremost, we would like to thank James Williams and Angela Corbin for allowing us to share their stories about attending college as students with disabilities. Your words will allow others to realize their own potential and seek the services they need to be successful college students. We also would like to thank our colleagues who have supported us through the writing process and encouraged us to move forward with our own dreams. Special thanks to Patricia Brautigam whose contributions and feedback strengthened the content of the book. Last, we would like to thank the Student Chapters of Council for Exceptional Children, specifically, the Sam Houston Chapter for Exceptional Children for your work with students with disabilities and your efforts in providing and welcoming college students with disabilities into your organization and onto the college campus.

INTRODUCTION

*College Planning for Students
With Learning Disabilities and
Other Special Needs*

THE high school years are an exciting time for students as they make plans for the future. Will I get a job? Will I go to college? Where will I live? Will I have friends? These are just a few of the questions that all students must face, but the answers may not always be easily accessible for students with special needs. Most high schools have career centers that provide students with a wealth of information on topics such as college information sessions, financial aid, scholarships, and required testing. In addition, an overwhelming amount of college-related mail is distributed to students throughout their high school years. Unfortunately, the information received does not specifically address students with disabilities or even what services are offered to help mediate the process called *college planning.*

The intent of this book is to serve as a resource for students, parents, teachers, and other professionals who will assist in the development of a strategic process that can be individualized for students with learning disabilities (LD), along with other disabilities, such as Attention Deficit Hyperactivity Disorder (ADHD) and Asperger's syndrome, who are transitioning from high school to college (also referred to as postsecondary education). Throughout the book, we often use the word "disabilities" or "disability" in lieu of identifying a specific disability. Although the content of the book clearly is geared toward the aforementioned disabilities, current practices within our public school system and within the field of special education have begun to identify students as those accessing the general education curriculum and those students who are not.

The use of Response to Intervention (RTI) as a means to identify students as having a specific learning disability creates the possibility of students with LD not being identified as having LD but rather as a student accessing the general education curriculum with academic supports. Response to Intervention is an alternative method of diagnosing LD to the ability-achievement discrepancy model, which requires students to display a significant discrepancy between their IQ and academic achievement based on the results of standardized tests (Shinn, 2007). RTI seeks to prevent failure through early intervention, frequent progress monitoring, and the use of intensive research-based instructional strategies. Data collected on these strategies are used to determine progress or additional need for more services.

Furthermore, this method of diagnostics may or may not leave the student as one identified under Section 504. If this is the case, the student may still receive accommodations in college even though he or she was not receiving special education services during the high school years. Thus, these changes in the identification process may pose challenges to a smooth transition into postsecondary education; however, the information gathered while using the RTI model also provide data that may be more recent and relevant to the student's abilities (Sitlington & Clark, 2006). The college can use this data in working with the student to determine needed accommodations to his or her program of study. Because public schools currently are in the process of moving to this identification process, the student may have to go to a private school psychologist to get the necessary documentation for his or her disability, which then may be requested by the college.

Therefore, to limit this book to only those identified as having a specific learning disability might leave the impression that students with other disabilities or students served under Section 504 would not benefit from the information presented throughout the book. Any students served under Section 504 or receiving special education services, regardless of the identified disability, will find helpful information for the transition process from high school to postsecondary education. This process has to begin at the secondary level or earlier so that the student is prepared to move into the college setting. Needless to say, the entire process can become quite daunting when searching for this information, so planning is essential!

This book provides a step-by-step guide that can be used to help chart the path toward planning for a postsecondary education. Each chapter ends with Chapter Resources that include a copy of the checklists referred to within the chapter. Students may copy the checklists, place them in a binder, and use them to keep detailed records of their own individual planning process. At the end of the book, a Resources Section provides information on financial aid and additional college planning resources.

Finally, each chapter of this book includes an interview with two students who will share their own experiences as college students with disabilities. Each of the students attends Sam Houston State University (SHSU) in Huntsville, TX. The first interview is with James Williams. James is currently a 21-year-old senior pursuing a degree in special education. He was identified with Asperger's syndrome at the age of 12. James shares his own experiences related to the content of each chapter and provides practical tips that guided him through the process.

The second interview is with Angela Corbin, who is majoring in early childhood education. She was diagnosed with a learning disability (specifically, a math disorder and a processing disorder), when she was 9 years old. Angela currently receives services as a student with LD. Although both of the students interviewed possess different disabilities, their experiences while attending college offer insights as to the obstacles they face attending college as students with disabilities and how they work to overcome the challenges presented to them. It is our goal that readers, regardless of their role in the college planning process, will be able to use this book as a roadmap to assist students with disabilities toward a successful college career.

The interest in writing this book began on a more personal level. After teaching in the public school setting and at the college level, we have had the opportunity to meet many students with disabilities who said they never pursued a college education because they did not realize that was an option for them. Some students stated that their teachers, school counselor, and parents never discussed the possibility of postsecondary education as being a viable option. Other students said that they had begun a college education, but they were unaware or unable to access the services they needed in order for them to be successful academically. Still, there were other students who were tired of being labeled with a disability in high school, so they chose not to self-identify once they were in college. Unfortunately, many of these students were unable to succeed without any supports in place.

It is our intent that this book be used as a resource that can inform students with disabilities that, firstly, they can pursue a college education; secondly, how to move forward with their goal of transitioning to college; and finally, that they are their own biggest advocate. Information is power, and we hope that we have been able to compile the necessary information that students will need in order to advocate for themselves and have a successful college experience.

MAKING THE CHANGE

Transition Planning

OVERVIEW OF THE TRANSITION PLANNING PROCESS

STEPHEN Covey said "to begin with the end in mind" (1989, p. 9). This quote summarizes the focus of transition planning. It sets the educational course for students to move successfully from school to postsecondary education, vocational training, integrated employment, independent living, and community participation based on the student's preferences, interests, and abilities. Most students who are planning a college education begin the process during the high school years. However, for students with disabilities, that process will need to begin much earlier. As a student with disabilities in the public school system, you are protected under certain laws that provide specific rights and responsibilities. However, once you have graduated from high school and move into a postsecondary institution, there are changes in the laws that will affect your rights and responsibilities, as well as the services that can be provided. It is important to know what these changes are and to begin addressing them long before graduation from high school.

Ensuring that students with disabilities have access to and full participation in postsecondary education has become a major focus in secondary education and transition planning for students with disabilities. Postsecondary education is targeted as an important transition outcome for students with disabilities because of the impact of a college degree on future adult outcomes (Madaus & Shaw, 2006). Students with disabilities who graduate from college have employment rates and salaries comparable to their peers without disabilities (National Center for Education Statistics, 2000). Thus, it seems imperative that students with disabilities, as well as their parents, teachers, and counselors, be well-informed on how to best prepare to pursue a postsecondary education, as well as learn the skills needed to be successful in that setting.

Over the past decade, an increasing number of students with disabilities have been choosing to pursue a postsecondary education. According to data from the National Longitudinal Transition Study 2, 76.7% of students with disabilities were planning to attend a postsecondary school when surveyed in high school (Newman, 2005). However, 2 years after high school, only 19% were attending a postsecondary school. In comparison, 40.5% of youth without disabilities were currently attending a postsecondary school. Data collected in 2003 for the National Longitudinal Transition Study 2 revealed that 3 in 10 youth with disabilities have been enrolled in some kind of postsecondary school since leaving high school (Newman, 2005).

Although these numbers are still low, the impact of federal policy calling for transition planning in the Education for All Handicapped Children Act Amendments of 1990, and the subsequent 1997 and 2004 amendments to the Individuals with Disabilities Education Improvement Act have resulted in improved transition services and have had a positive effect on better preparing students with disabilities for life after high school (Newman, 2005). These changes have encouraged students with disabilities to consider all of their options after high school, including college. It is the responsibility of students, parents, teachers, and other educational professionals to make sure we provide the information and support to make college a reality.

IEP PROCESS

As you begin to consider your future plans, it is essential that you become an active part of your own Individualized Education Program (IEP). According to the Individuals with Disabilities Education Act (IDEA; 2004), a statement of needed transition services that includes strategies and activities that will assist the student in preparing for postsecondary activities has to be included in the IEP at least by the time the child turns 16 years of age, and it must be updated annually (IDEA, 2004). The IEP must include:

> ▶ appropriate measurable postsecondary goals based upon age-appropriate transition assessments related to training, education, employment and, where appropriate, independent living skills;
> ▶ the transition services (including courses of study) needed to assist the child in reaching those goals; and
> ▶ beginning not later than one year before the child reaches the age of majority under state law, a statement that the child has been informed of the child's rights under IDEA, if any, that will transfer to the child on reaching the age of majority under Section 615(m). [614(d)(1)(A)(VIII)]

The term *transition services* refers to a coordinated set of activities for a child with a disability

> that (a) is designed to be within a results-oriented process, that is focused on improving the academic and functional achievement of the child with a disability to facilitate the child's movement from school to postschool activities, including postsecondary education, vocational education, integrated employment (including supported employment), continuing and adult education, adult

services, independent living or community participation; (b) is based on student's needs and taking into account the child's strengths, preferences, and interests; and, (c) includes instruction, related services, community experiences, the development of employment and other postschool adult living objectives, and, when appropriate, acquisition of daily living skills and functional vocational evaluations. In addition, services must be focused on improving academic and functional achievement, and must take into account the child's strengths. (IDEA, 2004, Section 602)

Certainly, the expansion of the federal law has required educators to be actively involved in addressing future goals and outcomes for students with disabilities. But, what does this look like in the school setting?

LEARNING TO ASK THE RIGHT QUESTIONS

1. Does your current IEP include appropriate measurable postsecondary goals?
2. Does your current IEP include a statement of transition services needed to meet the postsecondary goals?
3. If you have reached the age of 17, have you been informed that your rights under IDEA will be transferred to you upon reaching the age of majority, which is 18 years of age?
4. What role do you have in developing your own transition plan?

STUDENT-LED IEP MEETINGS

First of all, it is imperative that students be an active part of the IEP process as soon as possible. This is a judgment call that has to be made by your parents and the teachers and other school staff who are working with you on a regular basis. During your elementary years, you were probably not in attendance at the IEP meeting, but it is important that as you become older, your role in the IEP meeting moves from nonattendance, to observer, to active participant. If this is not the case in your school, you and your parents should contact your counselor and other school staff to make arrangements for your inclusion in these meetings.

Once you begin attending your own IEP meeting, Mason, McGahee-Kovac, and Johnson (2004) suggest three general levels for your participation, ranging from presenting limited information to assuming responsibility for all aspects of the IEP meeting.

> *Level 1:* Teachers and administrators still lead the IEP meeting, but you read or present information about your transition plan. In other words, you talk about what you want to do after high school and what steps you need to take while in high school to reach those goals.
>
> *Level 2:* Teachers and administrators still lead most of the meeting, but you explain your disability and how it affects your school performance, talk about your strengths and weaknesses, and explain the accommodations you need and prefer for success in the classroom.
>
> *Level 3:* At this level, you lead the entire IEP meeting. Although it initially may be easier for teachers and administrators to lead the IEP meeting, the benefits for you to take on this role can be significant. Leading the meeting gives you an opportunity to advocate for yourself, practice your communication skills, and build your own self-confidence. There are specific IEP meeting instructions that vary from school to school, and your teachers will be able to teach you this process as you become more involved and independent in participating in your IEP meeting.

PROVIDING STUDENT SUPPORT

Without specific IEP meeting instructions, students may not know what to do, understand the purpose of the meeting or what is being said, and feel as if no one is interested in what they have to say (Martin et al., 2006). Teaching you to lead the IEP meeting gives you more ownership in developing your own transition plan and encourages you to focus on future goals. The following are some of the steps involved in preparing students to become an active part of the actual process:

- ▶ Teach the IEP process and the components of the IEP.
- ▶ Teach the student about his or her own disability and how it affects him or her academically and physically.
- ▶ Have the student study his or her current IEP and meet with the assessment team to gain a better understanding of assessment results and how the results apply to his or her disability.
- ▶ Encourage the student to meet with the teacher and parents to develop a draft of his or her own IEP. This pre-IEP meeting will give the student an opportunity to communicate his or her own goals and objectives before the IEP meeting.

One of the most informative Web sites to help you prepare to be part of this process can be found at the National Dissemination Center for Children with Disabilities (http://www.nichcy.org/InformationResources/Pages/default.aspx). As you begin learning about the IEP process, the range of your involvement in the IEP meeting should increase. Eventually, you may be able to lead the entire meeting. Research shows that students who lead their IEP meetings increase their confidence, communication skills, leadership skills, and advocacy skills (Mason et al., 2004). These are skills that will provide lasting benefits for students who are pursuing a postsecondary education.

LEARNING TO ASK THE RIGHT QUESTIONS

1. What role do you have in your IEP meetings?
2. Do you understand the goals that are written on your IEP?
3. Do you understand the accommodations that are written on your IEP?
4. What information would assist you in preparing to lead your own IEP meeting?

TRANSITION TIMELINES

As stated in IDEA (2004), your IEP will need to include a statement of transition services as defined earlier in this chapter. This statement will be based upon your needs while taking into account your own preferences and interests. It will include:

- instruction,
- related services,
- community experiences,
- employment,
- independent living,
- acquisition of daily living skills (when needed), and
- functional vocational evaluation (when needed).

Developing the transition plan may include a number of people to ensure that all areas of the plan are addressed. You, and your family, special education teacher, guidance counselor, vocational educator, therapists, adult agency service providers, and other possible members that may be needed to plan for a smooth transition may be invited to participate. Again, the transition services must be based on your needs, preferences, and interests as a student to successfully meet the postsecondary outcomes. Academic decisions related to the required coursework will need to begin in the middle school years. You will want to make sure you are taking the courses that will fulfill the requirements of a postsecondary institution. The following sections provide information at each grade level to be used in the planning process, including checklists for your use.

EIGHTH GRADE

For the student who is planning for college, eighth grade is the year to discuss transition into high school with parents, the IEP team, and the guidance counselor. You will need to develop a master plan that will include the courses you will need for high school graduation and those you might need to attend community or 4-year colleges. Here are some actions you will want to take during your eighth-grade year:

- ▶ Obtain a copy of the high school course of study catalogue, or if this is not available, a listing of diploma requirements from the school counselor.
- ▶ Review the Web sites of possible postsecondary colleges you may be interested in so that you can become familiar with the course requirements for acceptance, as well as any entrance exams that may be required.
- ▶ Develop the high school course of study plan based on the requirements of the colleges in which you are interested. If you plan to attend a 2-year or 4-year college, the following high school courses usually are required:
  - English . . . . 4 years
  - Math . . . . 4 years
  - Natural Sciences . . . . 3 years
  - Social Studies. . . . . 3–4 years
  - Foreign Language . . . . 2–4 years

  Some colleges may recommend or require additional courses. For instance, if you are interested in attending an art school, you may need to add 4 years of art study to this slate of general coursework.
- ▶ If you do not already have a transition plan as part of your IEP, you and your parents should arrange to have it included at this time. You do not have to wait until the age of 16 to ask that the transition statement be included in your IEP.
- ▶ Develop study skills. You may want to take an extra study skills course or summer program to help you begin building these techniques early.

- ► Start saving money. Your parents can start looking into various savings plans for your education. You also might consider getting involved in contests, which often include scholarships, cash prizes, and savings bonds as awards. Saving personal money now can help you slowly put aside spending money for college.
- ► Remediate and/or compensate for basic skill deficits through tutoring or summer coursework.
- ► Turn to the Resources Section of this chapter to see an example of a Transition Planning Worksheet.

You will want to get a folder or binder to keep your Transition Planning Worksheet, course of study catalogue, and other important papers you are going to collect throughout the high school years. It is never too soon to start this folder, and it is a great way to keep important information together. This will ensure that everything needed for the college application process is located in one place and is easily accessible.

Because students with disabilities have an IEP, they are eligible to remain in the public school system through the age of 21. If this is your case, the next section may be extended over the 6–7 years that you remain at the high school level. However, this decision will be made in conjunction with you and your IEP team.

Ninth Grade

This typically is the beginning of the high school years and time to start thinking about the possibility of pursing a postsecondary education. There are certain actions you will need to take each year as you progress through high school so that you are prepared to transition into a college or university. You also may use this information as a guide or checklist to help you remain on track in preparing for life after high school. The following is a list of actions to take during your ninth-grade year of high school.

- ▶ Visit the high school career center; typically, it will have a wealth of information and resources available to help you begin looking at colleges and will provide many services for students with disabilities. Your career center counselor or advisor also has multiple career inventories and tests that can help you determine what your future field may be (which can affect the type of postsecondary schooling you will want to pursue).

- ▶ Develop skills for academic independence such as time management, study skills, and note-taking. This does not mean you shouldn't utilize available accommodations for these skills, but that you should make sure you begin to develop your own abilities in these areas and begin to recognize your strengths and weaknesses in these areas.

- ▶ Explore assistive technology tools and make sure you can use computer software including word processing and spreadsheets. Many tutorials for these software programs are available online.

- ▶ At the annual IEP meeting, make sure you are taking the required courses for high school graduation. Also, discuss any college entrance exams that might be required with the school counselor. The school counselor will need to complete the necessary paperwork to allow your identified testing accommodations to be used with these entrance exams. Your counselor also may be able to direct you to test prep programs that have worked well for other students in the past.

- ▶ Work with your school counselor to set up a plan for taking college entrance exams. These exams can be taken multiple times during your high school years. The SAT exam also offers practice tests during your 10th- and 11th-grade years. By making a schedule of when you will take these exams, you can be better prepared and make time for studying in advance. However, you need to know that if you are a student with a disability who receives testing accommodations as part of your IEP, you also will qualify for testing accommodations on college exams. To begin this process, visit the Educational Testing Service Web site at http://www.ets.org and click on "Test Takers with Disabilities."

► Explore and choose some of the extracurricular activities you want to become involved in during high school. This is important information that will be requested on all college applications, so you should keep a file that documents dates and activities in which you participate. Such activities also can lead you to other postsecondary opportunities you may have otherwise looked over—for example, a drama club or class may spark a talent for acting, pointing you toward a fine arts college.

► Explore options for completing some community service projects. Again, this information will be requested on all college applications, so a file should be kept that documents dates and activities throughout high school.

► Continue to remediate and/or compensate for basic skill deficits.

► Work hard in all of your classes, so you can keep up your GPA. Take advantage of teachers who offer extra study sessions or tutorials before and after school, as these may be good opportunities to get one-on-one time with your instructors.

Tenth Grade

Now that you have completed your first year of high school, you need to begin thinking about possible postsecondary options. The focus of your 10th-grade year will be much the same as the previous year, but there are also some additional actions that you need to pursue during this school year.

The following actions should be taken in the 10th-grade year:

- ► Review your 4-year plan and high school transcript with the IEP team and school counselor. At this point, if it is determined that any coursework is missing, you'll want to adjust your schedule or prepare for summer courses.
- ► Sign up for and take a practice college entrance exam. Remember to check out the Educational Testing Services Web site for information on testing accommodations for students with disabilities at http://www.ets.org.
- ► Visit a nearby college and talk with someone who works with students who have disabilities. All campuses should have an office that assists prospective and current students with disabilities. It also may be beneficial to talk with current university students with disabilities to get their advice on college planning.
- ► Continue your involvement in extracurricular activities and community service. This may be a good time to look at taking on leadership roles within those activities by offering to head up projects or work on committees.
- ► Continue academic preparation and remediation/compensation strategies and identify any assistive technology needs.
- ► Continue to work hard in all of your classes, so you can keep up your GPA. Also, keep taking advantage of any one-on-one time with your teachers—a good sophomore year does not mean that you should not continue successful work habits and strategies in the years to come.

ELEVENTH GRADE

Many high school counselors refer to the 11th-grade year as being the most important year for students pursuing a college education. It is during this year that a large number of students take their college entrance exams. Plus, when students begin completing college applications in the summer prior to their senior year or the fall semester of their senior year, the last full year of grades they have to submit is from their 11th-grade year. Therefore, you want to make sure you have a strong academic year and remain on track as you move closer to graduation.

During your 11th-grade year, you should take the following actions:

- Review your 4-year plan and high school transcript with the IEP team and school counselor. Make sure that you are still on track for graduation.
- Sign up for and take a college entrance exam. You also may consider taking a preparatory course for this exam in the semester before you take it or you can take free practice exams at http://www.smartaboutcollege.org. You should have already checked out the Educational Testing Services Web site for information on testing accommodations for students with disabilities at http://www.ets.org during the 10th-grade year, but there is still time if you act quickly.
- Attend College Night at your high school or a local college fair to obtain additional information from colleges in which you might be interested.
- Check out http://www.commonapp.org to see which colleges will accept the common application. You may begin completing this application at your convenience.
- Identify at least two teachers and two other people you could use as references on your college application. At least one of these persons should be from your community, either someone you have worked with in your community service, an employer, or a community leader, such as your religious leader or camp counselor.

- Begin visiting colleges you may be interested in attending. Take advantage of special visitation services such as campus tour guides. Make an appointment to talk with someone who works with students who have disabilities. It is important to find out what services the college provides for students with disabilities to help determine if the college is a match. Find current students with disabilities from whom you can receive advice and guidance.

- Continue your involvement in extracurricular activities and community service. Now is a great time to begin taking on leadership roles (no matter how small they may be). You also should keep in mind that solid participation and leadership in one or two activities can be just as significant on your application, if not more so, than minor membership or participation in multiple activities.

- Continue academic preparation and remediation/compensation strategies, assistive technology needs, and self-advocacy skills.

- Begin looking at and applying for scholarships independent from universities. Many exist for students with disabilities who wish to complete postsecondary educations. Resources for financial aid and scholarships can be found in the Resources Section at the end of this book.

- Prepare transition packets for disability documentation that include evaluation reports, transcripts, test scores, current IEP, medical records, writing samples, and letters of recommendation. You will want to work with your school counselor and/or administrators and administrative assistants to get official copies of some of these documents.

- Keep working hard in all of your classes, so you can keep up your GPA.

Figure 1 provides a copy of a comprehensive Junior Year Planning Checklist developed by college planning expert Sandra Berger (2006). Although this checklist originally was created for use with gifted students, its information has proven to be helpful to *all* students applying for college. You can review and modify this list with your parents and counselor, perhaps spreading some of its suggested actions across 2 years of school. Keep in mind that there are many lists like this one available. You should always modify such lists to match your needs and goals.

Twelfth Grade

This is not the year to stop working! The senior year is a busy time for students, and it can be difficult to remain focused academically. Even though you may have completed the application process to some colleges, the admissions office will request a copy of your final grades upon graduation. Colleges have been known to retract their offer of admission if there has been a significant decrease in your academic performance or extracurricular activities and community service.

In your final year of high school, you should take the following actions:

- ► Review your 4-year plan and high school transcript with the IEP team and school counselor. Has everything been completed so that you can graduate? Compensate for missing coursework by changing your schedule, if needed.
- ► Sign up for and take a college entrance exam if you are interested in raising your previous scores. Again, you may want to consider preparatory courses, especially if your goal is to raise your scores.
- ► Visit any colleges that you are still considering applying to, but remember that the deadlines typically occur in the fall of your senior year. You may want to do last-minute visits to colleges early in the year, or during the summer

The following calendar of college planning steps is a detailed checklist you can use to make sure you are on target for 11th and 12th grades:

___ Prepare a college planning portfolio that includes academic courses (including courses taken during the summer or after school), extracurricular activities, community service, achievements, and awards.

___ Make up a chart that can be used to keep track of dates and details. Your chart should include:

   ___ application deadlines (including early action and early decision dates);

   ___ financial aid deadlines (they are often different at different colleges);

   ___ notification dates;

   ___ tests required;

   ___ costs;

   ___ number and type of recommendations required;

   ___ interview deadlines and locations; and

   ___ dates for ACTS, SATs, and subject tests.

___ Save your writing samples. Some colleges ask to see all of the drafts, as well as the final product.

___ Develop a list of 10 to 20 colleges. Work up a comparison chart. Include factors that are important to you, and keep in mind the following factors:

   ___ size (campus, number of students);

   ___ geographic location (urban, rural, North, South, etc.);

   ___ course offerings (Do they teach what you like?);

   ___ cost (tuition, room and board, books, travel to and from home, etc.);

   ___ available scholarships or tuition assistance programs;

   ___ extracurricular activities (newspaper, sports, etc.); and

   ___ selectivity (degree of difficulty).

___ Some additional points to consider include:

   ___ curriculum and course requirements for specific majors;

Figure 1. Junior year planning checklist.

Note. From *College Planning for Gifted Students* (3rd ed., pp. 221–223), by S. L. Berger, 2006, Waco, TX: Prufrock Press. Copyright © 2006 by Prufrock Press. Reprinted with permission.

___ student life;

___ special programs (e.g., study abroad);

___ academic advising and career counseling procedures;

___ whether professors or teaching assistants teach freshman courses;

___ faculty-student relationships; and

___ student access to required readings, laboratory space, and computer terminals (e.g., Is the campus wireless? If not, are there enough terminals for everyone to use during peak periods, such as midsemester and final exams?).

___ Visit several colleges you are considering. Make sure that the colleges you want to visit will be in session, and call ahead for an appointment if you want an interview with an admissions officer.

___ Consider a summer activity such as:

___ local or university-based summer school (keyboarding, performing arts, computer programming, engineering, philosophy, etc.);

___ a summer internship;

___ school-sponsored travel;

___ courses offered by talent search programs (i.e., the opportunity to acquire college credits and try out a college lifestyle); or

___ a college planning seminar (offered by many colleges).

___ Ask for letters of recommendation from your supervisor, camp director, formal or informal mentor, or others before you complete your summer and school year activities. Do not wait until later. You want these people to write about you when they remember you best. Ask that the letters be addressed to "To Whom It May Concern," and give the letters to your guidance counselor as soon as possible. Keep copies.

___ Send away for application forms for 6 to 10 colleges.

___ Make appointments for personal interviews at colleges you plan to visit in the fall or winter.

___ Recheck application deadlines. Start filling out application forms early in the fall. Learn how to complete an error-free application. Make extra copies of each application form. Use the copies for practice before completing the originals.

___ Unless instructions say otherwise, type everything. If you can't type, consider using a computerized application. Have someone proofread every word on your application forms. Correct all errors.

___ Make and keep copies of everything.

before your senior year, if you need to narrow down your choices further.

- In preparation for the college application, you should work with your English teacher to complete your college essay. You also should line up time with another teacher or your counselor to proofread your essay.

- Continue your involvement with extracurricular activities and community service. Start thinking about which activities you would like to continue in college.

- Strengthen self-advocacy skills. You can take legal responsibility for your education at the age of 18.

- Apply for scholarships for the following year. Again, take notice of awards geared toward students with disabilities. You and your parents also should work with your school counselor to complete the Free Application for Federal Student Aid (FAFSA), so that you are eligible for grants and student loans. Keep in mind that if you do not fill out a FAFSA, you cannot receive federal aid. You also need to note if the schools you've applied to require this form to be completed before a certain date.

- Continue working hard in all of your classes so you can finish with a strong GPA. This may be more difficult during the senior year, because you naturally are ready to graduate, but you have to remember to stay focused.

- Once you receive acceptance, if you've received multiple acceptance letters, talk with your family and visit those schools to make a decision. Then, begin the planning process for attendance, including housing, travel arrangements, academic advising, and other necessities (many of which we will explain later in this book).

Although this is an exciting time for students, there is a great deal of planning that occurs prior to heading off to college. Make sure you keep current, accurate records and that your Transition Plan is updated annually so you remain on track.

LEARNING TO ASK THE RIGHT QUESTIONS

1. Are you using a Transition Planning Worksheet to make sure you are following a timeline to achieve your postsecondary goals?
2. Do you have a designated place to keep your Transition Planning Worksheet, course of study catalogue or copy of your 4-year plan, and other important papers that you are collecting while you are in high school?
3. Is your IEP updated at each IEP meeting to reflect the current status of your transition goals?

CONCLUSION

If you are a student with a disability who is considering a college education, the planning process has to begin early. Fortunately, the changes in the federal laws over the past two decades have given you a greater role and responsibility in planning for your future by making you an integral part of the IEP team and all of the decision-making responsibilities that are afforded the team. The days of being told what is included on your IEP should be behind you, because you should not only be actively involved in writing your IEP, but you may even be leading the meeting.

However, along with that expanded role you will play in developing your IEP, you can see that there are numerous steps involved in preparing for a postsecondary education. Beginning early will help pave the way for a smooth transition from high school to college. With the detailed information organized by grade level in this chapter, you can create a guideline or checklist to aid you in the planning process.

STUDENT INTERVIEWS

What steps did you take to begin the transition process during your high school years?

James: The first and most important step I took was to decide that I *wanted* to go to college and become a successful adult. As much as our parents may want us to attend college, as individuals with Asperger's syndrome and other disabilities, we must have the level of self-determination to make it happen. Both parents and school systems can and should provide us with the appropriate strategies; however, if we are not self-determined, success is difficult, if not, impossible to achieve. Another important step that I took was to begin researching my options both independently and with assistance. Agencies such as the Texas Department of Assistive and Rehabilitative Services provided some assistance in regard to referrals to other assistance. In reality, though, most of the assistance came from my parents and from my social coach at FOCUS Initiative, a for-profit organization that provides various services to individuals with Autism Spectrum Disorders. Again, my actions were always driven by my level of self-determination.

Angela: Throughout middle school and high school I had help from my parents, private tutoring, modifications such as fewer answer choices and extra time, and I went to Content Mastery. Once in high school, I saw a tutoring specialist once a week. I took the SAT test but scored too low to get into college, and my grades were not good either. Once it came close to the summer after high school, I realized I needed to do something and so I attended Houston Community College all summer and completed 13 hours of credit. I transferred into Sam Houston State University (SHSU) and was ready to begin in the fall. No one believed I would ever make it to college or complete college for that matter. They gave me options such as community colleges and told me about looking for a job. I was determined to get into SHSU and after a long summer of hard work I finally realized I could be successful and I was on my way.

What resources did you find most helpful in making plans to attend college?

James: The most helpful resources I found were usually located on the Internet. There is so much good information on the Internet regarding colleges, degrees, and career paths. I did have to know where to start and for that information I asked my brother, who was already in college, and my counselor's office. There was a lot of good information available through my local library, as well, and I found it to be a good place to dig in and get information. I also found good information through some of my local state agencies, although the information was hard to find and at sometimes confusing. Honestly, this part of my transition was probably the most difficult due to the fact that there were very few places that you could find an organized batch of information. Because of this, I recently started a transition resource Web page called Transition Matters that provides documents and links to information regarding postsecondary transition for students with Asperger's syndrome or high functioning autism (see http://www.transitionmatters.org). This Web site consolidates many of the resources I have found helpful in addressing my own transition needs.

Angela: I had two older sisters who had both attended 4-year colleges and had been aware of the process by watching them go through it. My older sister is dyslexic. I watched how hard she worked and saw that she succeeded. She had found that the teachers at SHSU would work with her and were more personable, unlike another university from which she had transferred. I also made a lot of phone calls myself to seek additional information. The calls I made were mainly to the student center at the university. My parents also were very supportive and always kept the standards high for me. They believed in me.

What would be your recommendations on finding a college that can address a student's specific needs?

James: First, I would develop a plan that includes my future goals. Then I would take those goals and use them as a starting point. Although the design may vary by state, I would hope that most high school transition plans would include these goals and steps to achieve them. The key point to remember, though, is that IDEA only requires a plan to be written when the student reaches the age of 16, and many students would greatly benefit from an informal plan being written at an earlier age. For example, I wanted to become a special education teacher and go to a school within 3 hours of my parents' home. So, I compiled a list of all of the schools that offered that degree. Then, I went to the university Web sites and began narrowing my choices. I contacted both the Services for Students with Disabilities Coordinator and the College of Education Dean's Office to learn more about what they offered. Based on that information, I scheduled personal visits. A strong indicator that you have found a supportive environment is the "culture" or attitude of the campus. The term *culture* is used to describe the willingness of an institution to provide accommodations to students with disabilities, as well as the quality of those accommodations. An institution with a good culture would be one that educates its faculty and staff about disabilities, provides services that exceed the minimum required, and strives to welcome and actively recruit students with disabilities to its campus. For example, a college can be grounded in tradition, but still be progressive and proactive in its effort to assist and promote the attendance of individuals with disabilities.

Angela: Talk to people who already attend the colleges and make college visits. Make a list of questions and answer them for each prospective college, as well as a pro and con list for each school.

MIDDLE/HIGH SCHOOL
TRANSITION PLANNING WORKSHEET

Name _____ Date _____

Campus _____ Class of _____

Postsecondary Goal(s):

❑ Community College   ❑ 4-Year University
❑ Technical School   ❑ Job Placement   ❑ Other

❑ Minimum High School Program Requirements
   (# of credits specific to each school)

❑ Recommended High School Program Requirements
   (# of credits specific to each school)

Use the chart on the next page to track the student's completion of the required credits.

_____   _____

Student's Signature   Date

_____   _____

Parent's Signature   Date

_____   _____

Staff Member's Signature   Date

MIDDLE/HIGH SCHOOL TRANSITION PLANNING WORKSHEET, CONTINUED

Subject Areas/Credits Required	7th Grade	8th Grade	9th Grade	10th Grade	11th Grade	12th Grade	Total

WEB SITES RELATED TO CHAPTER 1

NATIONAL DISSEMINATION CENTER
FOR CHILDREN WITH DISABILITIES

http://www.nichcy.org/Pages/Home.aspx

This site serves as a central source of information on legal issues, laws, and research-based educational practices for children with disabilities.

NATIONAL SECONDARY TRANSITION
TECHNICAL ASSISTANCE CENTER

http://www.nsttac.org

The center helps support and improve transition planning services and outcomes for youth with disabilities, disseminate information, and provide technical assistance on scientifically based research practices.

EDUCATIONAL TESTING SERVICE

http://www.ets.org

This site provides information on accessing accommodations on college entrance exams for students with disabilities. Click on the "Test Takers with Disabilities" link for more information.

SMART ABOUT COLLEGE

http://www.smartaboutcollege.org

This site provides free ACT and SAT practice exams, plus information on paying for college, resources, and a hotline.

THE COMMON APPLICATION

http://www.commonapp.org

This site includes an online application that is used by many post-secondary schools to promote access by evaluating students using a holistic selection process. The application forms can be obtained at this site, both online and in print.

Transition Matters

http://www.transitionmatters.org

This site provides documents and links to information regarding postsecondary transition for students with Asperger's syndrome or high functioning autism.

CHAPTER
TWO

[STAND UP FOR YOURSELF]

Advocacy

KNOWING YOUR RIGHTS AND RESPONSIBILITIES

As the number of students with disabilities who are entering and graduating from postsecondary institutions continues to increase (Eckes & Ochoa, 2005), it is imperative that such students know what services are available, as well as the process to access these services. Understanding the law is a critical component in planning for a smooth transition into a postsecondary institution. Without this information, you may not receive all of the services that the educational system, both secondary and postsecondary institutions, is required to provide. Students, parents, and educators of students with disabilities have to be knowledgeable and proactive in making sure that information is accessible and accurate. Keeping current on changes within the state and federal laws may have a significant impact on the information that is included in your transition plan.

FEDERAL LAWS: IDEA, ADA, SECTION 504

While in the public school system, students with disabilities are provided services based on the Individuals with Disabilities

Education Improvement Act (IDEA; 2004). Under IDEA, school districts are required to provide a free appropriate education to students with disabilities based on their individualized educational needs. The services may include an educational setting within a continuum of special education placements, and accommodations and modifications to the regular education program including adjustments in test-taking procedures, assignments, and grading, as well as related services such as physical therapy (Gil, 2007).

Students not covered under IDEA 2004 may be covered under Section 504 of the Rehabilitation Act of 1973 (Section 504) and the Americans with Disabilities Act of 1990 (ADA). Section 504 and ADA are civil rights laws that provide equal access and opportunity and prevent discrimination. However, once a student completes the 12th grade, IDEA 2004 is no longer applicable in the educational setting; therefore, services for students with disabilities in postsecondary institutions are provided under Section 504 and ADA. In most cases, postsecondary disability service providers interpret Section 504 and ADA guidelines to mean that a specific diagnosis with a clearly established functional limitation in a major life activity is required (National Joint Committee on Learning Disabilities [NJCLD], 2007).

Public colleges and universities generally receive federal financial assistance. There are some private colleges and universities that do not receive any federal assistance; therefore, Section 504 does not apply to them. When you are researching private postsecondary institutions, it will be necessary to inquire whether or not they receive federal assistance.

Table 1 provides a comparison of the rights and responsibilities between secondary and postsecondary education for students with disabilities. In addition, the U.S. Department of Education's Office for Civil Rights (2007) has posted a document on its Web site that will assist students in identifying important issues as they make the transition from high school to college (see http://www.ed.gov/about/offices/list/ocr/transition.html).

As is evident by the information in Table 1, changes in the rights and responsibilities you will be expected to carry out when moving from high school to a postsecondary institution are significant. The responsibility shifts from the school to the student. Therefore, as a college-bound student, you need to have a repertoire of specific skills that will prepare you to take on such responsibility and overcome transition challenges.

FAMILY EDUCATION RIGHTS AND PRIVACY ACT

Student records also are private and are protected by the Family Educational Rights and Privacy Act (FERPA), which was established in 1974 to protect the confidentiality of student medical and disability records. Disability records typically are kept by the university disabilities office. Files often are stored in secured files with access limited to appropriate personnel. FERPA protects you by not allowing your records to be shared with any party without your consent. This includes the faculty, your parents, administrators, and public entities such as the press.

LEARNING TO ASK THE RIGHT QUESTIONS

1. Do you have a basic understanding of your rights and responsibilities as a student with disabilities in high school?
2. Do you have a basic understanding of how your rights and responsibilities as a student with disabilities change after you complete high school and move into a college or university setting?
3. Do you know where to find answers to questions you might have regarding your rights and responsibilities as a student with disabilities?

Table 1

The Rights and Responsibilities of Students With Disabilities in Secondary and Postsecondary Education

Secondary Education	Postsecondary Education
Students Are Protected by: IDEA (2004) Section 504 ADA	**Students Are Protected by:** Section 504 ADA
Responsibilities for Identification and Evaluation: The school district is responsible for the identification and evaluation at the district's expense.	**Responsibilities for Identification and Evaluation:** The student must self-identify and provide documentation of a disability at his or her own cost.
Service Delivery: School districts are responsible for providing special education programs and services as identified in the student's IEP. The IEP team will decide on issues of placement, accommodations, or modifications and it may be necessary to alter a program or curriculum in order for the student to be successful. School districts must provide personal services when noted in the student's IEP, including assistive technology, transportation, and personal attendants.	**Service Delivery:** Students are responsible for notifying the Disability Support Services staff of their disability to discuss reasonable accommodations. Accommodations are provided in order for students with disabilities to have equal access to all programs and activities, but the essential program requirements are not altered. Postsecondary institutions are not responsible for providing any services that are not available to all students.
Enforcing the Law: The IEP team or the school professional in charge of the student's 504 plan is required to oversee the implementation of the student's services. IDEA is enforced by the Office of Special Education and Rehabilitative Services in the U.S. Department of Education, while Section 504 and ADA are civil rights statues overseen by the Office of Civil Rights and the U.S. Department of Justice in conjunction with the Equal Employment Opportunity Commission (EEOC).	**Enforcing the Law:** The student is responsible for asking the Disability Support Services staff to provide letters notifying professors of approved accommodations. Section 504 and ADA are civil rights statues overseen by the Office of Civil Rights and the U.S. Department of Justice in conjunction with the Equal Employment Opportunity Commission (EEOC).
Advocacy: Parents or guardians are the primary advocates for a student's needs.	**Advocacy:** Students must advocate for their own academic needs and services.

ADVOCACY IN ACTION

Clearly, there are a number of skills that students with disabilities need for a successful transition, but the foundation for these skills needs to be formed during the middle and high school years. Once a student leaves the public school and moves into an institution of higher education, he or she must advocate for his or her own academic needs and services. Therefore, at this transition point, as the student, you need to be able to make decisions and determine the path of your college career. This is a pivotal and critical part of a student's life. Legally, colleges and universities cannot share pertinent information regarding your academic progress to your parents unless a release of information authorizing your parents to access this information is secured. Nevertheless, you will need to advocate for yourself.

Self-advocacy can be defined as "the ability to act on what the individual knows about his or her needs, even though people may not offer the individual a clear choice or ask the individual to state his or her needs" (Van-Belle, Marks, Martin, & Chun, 2006, p. 40).The importance of teaching or helping individuals to realize the need to self-advocate is of growing concern. More and more students with disabilities are entering into the college setting with little or no skills in the area of self-advocacy. Most students are not taught these skills during their high school years and often students do not realize the need to obtain self-advocacy skills.

When students enter the college setting they move from a system designed to include a large degree of parental involvement (in other words, the student's disability is managed by someone else), to one built on student independence. For example, parents attend the IEP meeting and the IEP team determines IEP objectives and accommodations, but in college, you must determine and ensure that you receive accommodations. The change to being responsible for your education might seem overwhelming to you, but you are not alone:

> Unfortunately, the autonomy that the Family Education Rights and Privacy Act promotes is a shock to many students. Add to this surprise the reality that the major tenets of disability legislation for higher education (Section 504 of the Rehabilitation Act and the Americans with Disabilities Act) call for equal access, not guaranteed academic success, and it is no wonder that many students find the task of self advocacy overwhelming. (McCarthy, 2007, p. 12)

In part, that is why books such as this one can be so important to your college career. We recommend that all students with disabilities seek out local programs offered through universities that specifically address self-advocacy skills. Many programs will target those skills necessary to successfully advocate for oneself at the college level. Essential components of an effective self-advocacy skills program include:

1. Keep it simple. Know your own disability and how it affects your learning.
2. Learn your legal rights under IDEA, Section 504, and ADA.
3. Determine reasonable accommodations directly related to your disability.
4. Become more independent.
5. Create effective study patterns.
6. Manage your time.
7. Practice and role play effective self-advocacy skills.

If you are unable to attend specific workshops geared toward self-advocacy skills, you can begin to develop self-advocacy skills by taking responsibility for your actions. It is recommended that students need to understand their disability and how it affects them, their learning style, and their strengths and weakness, and have study skills and compensatory strategies (Gil, 2007). The following is a list of information that you will need to be able to communicate to those who are a part of your educational program. You need to be able to:

- ▶ explain the disability and your specific needs, and practice sharing this information with your teachers and parents;
- ▶ identify your areas of strengths and needs, both academic and physical (e.g., Do you have good computer skills? Do you have strong verbal skills? Are you a good athlete?);
- ▶ request needed accommodations and discuss changes that need to be made with your school's disabilities coordinator or counselor if these accommodations are not working;
- ▶ explain your legal rights and responsibilities (in some college classes, you may be more informed than your instructor regarding the laws that apply to students with disabilities in the academic setting, therefore, you need to be well-informed and have accurate legal information);
- ▶ schedule meetings with your professors to discuss accommodations and academic progress (remember, professors prefer to hear from students before they are failing the class); and
- ▶ realize that you are responsible for your life choices!

SELF-DETERMINATION

Self-advocacy is the ability to communicate one's talents, skills, and needed accommodations to others, while self-determination is defined as a combination of skills, knowledge, and beliefs that enable a person to engage in goal-directed, self-regulated, autonomous behavior. (Field, Martin, Miller, Ward, & Wehmeyer, 1998, p. 2)

Basically, self-determination emphasizes the development of skills and attitudes that enable individuals to become change agents in their own lives, making wise choices that increase the likelihood of achieving their desired goals (Wehmeyer, 1996). People who are self-determined tend to make things happen. They set goals and pursue them. "Self determination enables individuals to take responsibilities for their lives by defining and accomplishing goals" (Bashir, Goldhammer, & Bigaj, 2000, p. 52).

Research shows that self-determination may play a role in improving student outcomes, including academic performance, employment, postsecondary participation, and independence (Field, Sarver, & Shaw, 2003; Martin et al., 2003; Wehmeyer & Palmer, 2003). As a result, promoting students' self-determination has become an important component of best practices in the education of students with disabilities.

As you enter into the college setting, you must have a clear understanding of your own limitations, needs, and abilities. This understanding will provide the basis for the development of self-determination. Wehmeyer (2002) identified seven components in which educators can promote student self-determination, which you can use to help you develop this skill. These included:

- setting personal goals,
- solving problems that act as barriers to achieving these goals,
- making appropriate choices based on personal preferences and interests,
- participating in decisions that impact the quality of your life,
- advocating for yourself,
- creating action plans to achieve goals, and
- self-regulating and self-managing day-to-day actions.

As you begin to take a more active role in your own educational program and transition planning, it is essential that you have the opportunity to practice with some of your teachers while you are still attending public school. This practice is important because

> unfortunately, all too often students with disabilities enter post-secondary programs lacking understanding of how their disability affects their learning. As a result they are unable to effectively articulate the services and supports needed to meet the academic challenges in college. (Getzel & Thoma, 2008, p. 83)

In order to assist you with this task, a Self-Advocacy Skills Worksheet can be found in the Resources Section of this chapter to help you identify and discuss your own educational needs.

STAYING IN COLLEGE

Who are the students who complete their college education? In an examination of previous research, students with LD may have difficulty completing their postsecondary education (Murray, Goldstein, Nourse, & Edgar, 2000). Murray et al. collected data for postsecondary school attendance and completion rates during the first 10 years following high school for students with and without LD. Results showed that of the students with LD who had attended postsecondary education institutions, 80% had not graduated 5 years after high school, compared to 56% of youths without disabilities.

We are not suggesting that students with disabilities cannot be successful in postsecondary education, but whether or not to pursue a college education depends on the student's life goals. There also is the reality that some colleges are more "student friendly" than others (Sitlington & Clark, 2006). More information on knowing which colleges tend to work more collaboratively with students with disabilities can be found in Chapter 4.

Furthermore, research also has shown that there are certain characteristics that tend to be found in students who are successful in college, including students with disabilities. In 1997, Hicks-

Table 2

Comparing Successful and Unsuccessful Students

Factors	Successful Students	Unsuccessful Students
Motivation	Goal-oriented	Lack of goals
	Self-disciplined	Lack of self-discipline
	Determined	In school to please others
	Willingness to work hard	Procrastinates
Preparation	Academically prepared	Lack of academic preparation
	Knowledge of study skills	
	Knowledge of learning style	Lack of knowledge of study skills and learning style
	Time management skills	Lack of time management
	Believes he can succeed	Learned helplessness
Self-advocacy	Self-awareness	Unrealistic expectations
	Self-acceptance	Denial of disability
	Knowledge of laws, policies, and legal rights	Lack of knowledge of resources
	Assertiveness skills	Lack of self-esteem
	Problem-solving skills	Lack of problem-solving skills
		Lack of communication skills

Coolick and Kurtz interviewed the directors of the Learning Disabilities Support Services from nine postsecondary schools— two private universities, two state universities, two public 4-year colleges, one community college, and two vocational schools—to examine the personal characteristics that contribute to postsecondary academic success of students with LD. Results of their study revealed that motivation, preparation, and self-advocacy were the three determining factors of success.

Table 2 shows the characteristics that were identified under each factor for successful and unsuccessful students (Murray et al., 2000, p. 40).

For students with specific disabilities, immaturity may be a factor, and it may be better to postpone school for a year or two to allow the student some time to mature and gain some life experience. For example, a characteristic of ADHD is immaturity, and this may impact a student's decision to enter college immediately after the completion of high school or delay admittance. Again, this is a personal decision that needs to be made based on input from the IEP team, which hopefully includes the student.

Many students with disabilities have successfully completed a college education and made some excellent career choices. With a willingness to work hard, remain focused, understand your own learning style, and advocate for your needs, you can be one of those successful students. Remember, you are the key to your success!

LEARNING TO ASK THE RIGHT QUESTIONS

1. Do you understand your disability and how if affects you in the classroom?
2. Can you identify your academic strengths and weaknesses?
3. Do you know your learning style and what accommodations you need for academic success?
4. Do you know what strategies work the best for you in completing academic work?
5. Are you able to communicate your academic needs to your teachers, parents, and fellow students?

CONCLUSION

As a student with a disability, knowing and understanding the law may not be a topic you have spent a lot of time on, but it is definitely a critical component in making sure that the laws regarding transition planning are being implemented within your own IEP. Reading and understanding the information in Table 1 that identifies the differences in the rights and responsibilities between secondary and postsecondary schools will provide you with a clear overview of what you should expect from your IEP team and the school in regard to your own educational planning process.

Beyond the level of understanding comes the responsibility of self-advocating. With your increased involvement in understanding and participating in your transition plan, you will need to know how to explain your disability, identify and express your own strengths and areas of need, discuss your accommodations with your teachers and professors, and know what and how to address those in authority when questions arise regarding your academic program. Keeping current on the state and federal laws and how they impact you as a student with a disability will prepare you to advocate for yourself and ensure that your program is designed and implemented according to the law.

STUDENT INTERVIEWS

Were you involved in the process of developing your IEP in high school and did you attend your own IEP meetings? If so, what was your role in those meetings?

Angela: Yes, I attended and dreaded every moment of them. I hated that everyone involved would talk about you as if you were not sitting there. Some teachers would even use this time to inform my parents of things I had not completed or did poorly on. My role was to sit there and listen to them discuss me. I was asked over and over if I had any questions and helped to determine if there were any other accommodations that I thought would be useful. Then, at the end, they would ask me if what had been decided was OK with me and I would give my signature.

How much information did you know regarding your rights and responsibilities as a student with a disability entering a postsecondary institution?

James: At first, I wasn't sure of my rights because most of my knowledge was about IDEA, and my school did little, if anything, to keep me informed of my rights under the American with Disabilities Act or Section 504 of the Rehabilitation Act. Although I understand this is due in part to the relative infancy of college transition, I feel we should do much more to educate students with disabilities prior to their arrival on a college campus. I did not begin to fully understand my rights until my freshman year [of college], when I encountered a situation regarding my accommodations. Because of my training in becoming a special educator, I knew where to start looking, and I found most of my answers through the U.S. Department of Education's Office for Civil Rights. However, if I did not have my background in education, I would have had no idea where to start or what to do. The best way to remedy this is to use the point in an IEP meeting where rights are transferred to an adult student to discuss the protections that will be offered to the student in college. Even a self-determined student will find it hard to defend and understand his rights in higher education without significant assistance from parents, educators, or advocates. With that in mind, this process should begin as early as possible with significant emphasis placed on practice of your self-advocacy.

Angela: At first I only went to the disability office because my mom insisted that I go and get help. She left me with no choice. Once I went and started the process of getting accommodations, I became most interested in my learning disabilities. I finally realized that college was going to be extremely hard and I knew I had to prove to people and myself that I could complete the college coursework. I wouldn't say that I knew much more than high school about my rights and responsibilities for college, but I learned a lot going through the process of testing for my disability and setting up my accommodations through the university.

Were you knowledgeable about the laws regarding your rights and responsibilities as a student with a disability in high school?

Angela: No, not much at all, but my mom did. I felt that my parents as well as teachers sheltered me from my disability and so there was not a whole lot of information given to me besides what I needed to know to get the help needed on my work. To be honest, though, I wasn't really interested in knowing what was wrong with me either. It just seemed like everything was so hard.

Did that knowledge affect your decision in choosing a college?

James: In some ways, this knowledge did affect my ability to choose a college. I purposefully tried to choose campuses that seemed open to students with disabilities and was up front about our rights. In other words, they viewed their provision of accommodations as a positive and mutually beneficial practice, rather than an obligation mandated under federal law. Although all schools must offer basic accommodations as recipients of federal financial aid, many choose to offer more extensive accommodations and special services in an attempt to attract students with disabilities, which further diversifies their campus and provides equal access to their programs.

What are your recommendations on knowing your rights and responsibilities?

James: The first and most important step in understanding your rights and responsibilities is to read about the basic ideas behind both the Americans with Disabilities Act and Section 504 of the Rehabilitation Act. The laws are confusing and wordy, but several agencies, including the Department of Education's Office for Civil Rights, provide simplified pamphlets and resources on the main ideas. Using that knowledge, brainstorm a list of reasonable accommodations that you believe would enable you to successfully complete the courses your degree requires. Use this knowledge to request accommodations and assistance from your college. If your school's disabilities services office approves certain accommodations and one of your instructors/professors refuses or seems unwilling to provide them, self-advocate your needs with that professor and handle it in a polite and professional manner. If there is no progress, then it is important that you contact your SSD office and explain the situation. When you do this, keep two things in mind: Approved accommodations are legally protected/enforceable and you are never required to share your diagnosis with a professor or anyone else if you do not wish to. You are required to disclose your disability to your SSD office if you wish to have accommodations, but you don't have to defend or explain your disability to anyone who refuses to provide those accommodations."

How did you know that you would have to meet with the Academic Resource Center?

Angela: During my senior year of high school, my teachers made it clear that if I were to want further help after high school then I would have to seek it on my own. Once I got to college, I did a lot of searching myself until I found where I needed to go and what I needed to do.

SELF-ADVOCACY SKILLS WORKSHEET

Hi. I'm _____, and I am a student with _____
         (name)

_____ .

That means_____

_____

_____

_____

My academic strengths are: _____

_____

_____

_____

My areas of academic need are:_____

_____

_____

_____

Some accommodations I need for the classroom are:_____

_____

_____

_____

As a student with a disability, I am provided services under IDEA, Section 504, and ADA. IDEA is a federal law that grants rights to students with disabilities in the public school setting. IDEA will not apply once I am in college. However, Section 504 and ADA are civil rights laws that provide equal access and opportunity, and prevent discrimination and do apply when I am in college.

WEB SITES RELATED TO CHAPTER 2

NATIONAL CENTER ON SECONDARY EDUCATION AND TRANSITION: KEY PROVISIONS ON TRANSITION

http://www.ncset.org/publications/related/ideatransition.asp

This document identifies the major changes between IDEA 1997 and IDEA 2004 concerning transition services.

STUDENTS WITH DISABILITIES PREPARING FOR POSTSECONDARY EDUCATION: KNOW YOUR RIGHTS AND RESPONSIBILITIES

http://www.ed.gov/about/offices/list/ocr/transition.html

Information is provided to assist parents and students with disabilities regarding their rights and responsibilities during the transition process.

WRIGHTSLAW

http://www.wrightslaw.com

This Web site provides legal information regarding transition issues and students with disabilities.

CHAPTER
THREE

$$\Bigg[\quad \textbf{COLLEGE AS}\atop \textbf{THE NEXT STEP}\quad \Bigg]$$

THE journey after high school brings many challenges for students with and without disabilities. For a student with a disability, these challenges often are faced with higher levels of uncertainty especially when determining whether or not postsecondary education is a realistic and obtainable goal. The decision should not be one that is made in haste, but rather made after careful consideration. Parents often ask whether or not their child should attend college. Unfortunately, as with students without a specific disability, the answer to the question cannot be answered without carefully analyzing the particular strengths and areas of need that each student has. Comparing a student's ability to the expectations of selected colleges should be a critical factor in the decision-making process. Students with LD should consider the entire continuum of postsecondary education, including 2- and 4-year colleges, vocational/technical schools, GED programs, and adult education programs (Shaw, 2008).

Many students and families, including those students with disabilities, seek clarification of differences between 2- and 4-year postsecondary institutions. Many students with disabilities often attend community college for their first or only postsecondary education experience (Savukinas, 2003). Community colleges typically offer programs leading to the acquisition of a 2-year associate degree. In addition, certificate programs often are offered at the community college level. Many 4-year institutions have developed college transfer agreements with local community colleges. These agreements provide a basic listing of transferable courses offered at the community college level and specify the corresponding 4-year university course for which it will substitute. If you intend to transfer coursework to a 4-year institution, you should meet with an advisor at the community college prior to taking coursework to determine which courses would be considered college transfer courses at the 4-year institution you plan to attend.

In addition to a 2-year or community college, you may choose to attend a 4-year college or university starting with your freshman year. Most require that students seek a bachelor's degree in which they select a specific area of study or major. Four-year institutions tend to be more expensive than community colleges. Most 4-year institutions will offer specific career option certifications or licensures such as teaching or social work.

SELECTING A COLLEGE

After making the decision to attend a college or university for postsecondary education, the next obstacle ahead involves the selection of a college that best matches your individual needs. This selection should not be made solely on whether or not the college has a strong Student Disability Services Office, but rather it should be inclusive of the disability services offerings along with several other factors. You must examine your own needs and preferences in a variety of areas, including academics, social opportunities, and financial needs. Determining your specific needs should be done prior to completing the Postsecondary Preference Worksheet

(see the Resources Section of this chapter). A self-needs assessment involves examining critical questions involving your level of self-motivation and independence. Sandler (2008) identifies six questions to assess self-motivation and independence in students with ADHD that can be adapted to any disability:

1. Did you need support and structure in high school?
2. Do you routinely need help from others to keep you motivated and focused?
3. Do you thrive on individual attention from teachers?
4. Do you prefer to immerse yourself in a subject?
5. Do you need a high-energy environment?
6. Do you have trouble falling asleep?

Considerations of these questions will help guide you in completing the Postsecondary Preference Worksheet that can be found at the end of this chapter. Completion of this worksheet will allow you to identify those specific attributes that you desire in a college setting.

Along with an examination of needs and preferences, you should be considering the location of the college campus, exploring career goals, researching college options, examining the school's disability services, visiting college campuses, and most importantly, learning to ask the right questions. In progressing through each of these areas, students and parents often lose sight of the fact that college life extends beyond a student's academic needs. Careful planning for and exploring of college opportunities will enable you to receive not only academic achievement, but also social acceptance and extracurricular participation.

As you make decisions about which colleges to apply to, you should remember that there are a variety of resources available to students to help them in selecting a college that best matches their specific needs and desired preferences. Specific sources of information may include speaking with a school counselor, searching current information on the Internet (use specific search words such as locations you're interested in or types of schools you want, like vocational colleges), college guides obtained from local bookstores, college and universities admission offices, and lastly, the utilization of a specialized private college counselor. The use of a specialized college counselor can be expensive, but may be a good investment (Nadeau, 2006). The use of a specialized college counselor proves beneficial to students who need assistance with the application process, disability management, crisis intervention, and grievance processes. Those students who have heavily relied on parents often view the specialized college counselor as an element of their support system.

LOCATION OF COLLEGE CAMPUS

Determining whether or not the location of the college campus should be a priority in selecting a college to attend will be dependent on several factors including financial costs, easy accessibility to current medical providers, the student's ability to maintain relationship with family and friends within a specific mile radius, and/or access to transportation. Moving away from home can be difficult for all students regardless of whether or not they have a disability. However, some students with specific disabilities may face higher levels of anxiety or may not have the capability to live independently. If you do not feel you have the capability to live independently, it is possible that specific living skills can be identified and addressed prior to the college transition. If you will need a great deal of support from your family, it may be best to explore those college campuses that are within a close driving distance to the family home.

If you do not have the capability or financial means to live on a college campus, you should not rule out college attendance. Selecting a college within a convenient distance from your home will enable you to commute to and from campus while still receiving the necessary supports at home. You may want to consider beginning with a community college for a year or two to save money, then transferring to a 4-year school.

LEARNING TO ASK THE RIGHT QUESTIONS

1. Do you want to live on the college campus or commute to and from campus?
2. If you choose to live at home, how far of a commute is it to the college of your choice, and is public transportation available?
3. Is the college located in a small town or larger city? Will this impact your decision to attend?
4. Where are the parking facilities located? If your disability will require you to park in handicapped parking spaces, where are they located in relation to the building where the program of study you are interested in is housed?

EXPLORING CAREER GOALS

Once you determine that college should be the next step in your education, you also must examine what it is that you hope to obtain from attending college. Logically, it would be hopeful that you are attending postsecondary education in order to seek employment or move forth in career planning. Answering this question and specifically identifying your long-term goal is an important factor in selecting a college. However, once the decision is made, it is possible that you may change your mind after the first, second, or third year of college. In fact, students without disabilities often find themselves in this same situation. With this in mind, it is still important to recognize the goals that you have for yourself and select colleges to explore that offer the programming to meet these goals. For example, if you plan to become a graphic designer, it would be important to narrow down colleges and further examine those institutions that offer a degree in this area.

Most high school guidance counselors are well versed in the career planning processes. High school transition specialists also will address career goals during the transition planning of the IEP meeting (see Chapter 1 for additional information regarding the high school transition planning process). College and career fairs are excellent ways to explore career options. It is not necessary to choose your future career at this point, but it is important to begin thinking about areas in which you might be interested for the future.

LEARNING TO ASK THE RIGHT QUESTIONS

1. What degree is needed in order to reach the career path that you have selected?
2. Does the college you are investigating offer a program of study that matches your career goals?
3. Are there specific prerequisite high school courses that must be taken to enter into the program of study that matches your career goals?
4. Do your skills and interests match your career goal?
5. Will specific disability-related obstacles prevent you from reaching your career goal?

COST OF COLLEGE ATTENDANCE

Many families find themselves negotiating the college selection process based on the specific tuition and expenses of the college. Most private colleges or universities have higher tuition rates. However, for a student with a disability, there are several benefits that can be received from a private university. Private colleges and universities tend to have lower student-to-instructor ratios. Individuals with unique learning needs may benefit greatly from more personal contact with the faculty member teaching the course. Loans, scholarships, grants, and other means of financial aid may assist in making the attendance at a private university or college possible. Of course, smaller public institutions of higher learning will offer similar ratios, typically at a more affordable cost.

Financial aid offices are established to assist students in completing applications and determining which form of aid is needed.

Parents often express concern that because their child has a disability, he or she may not be eligible for scholarships or other gifts and awards. In many cases, scholarships are linked to academic or athletic performance. However, there is a vast array of scholarships with unique criteria including ethnicity, religion, extracurricular involvement, and/or community-based involvement. An excellent resource for finding financial aid options is http://www.heath.gwu.edu. This Web site specifically addresses financial aid for students with disabilities under "Creating Options: Financial Aid for Students with Disabilities."

For students with disabilities, Vocational Rehabilitation (VR) agencies offer funding and additional services that are geared toward training for employment, such as college. Individuals with disabilities have unique VR needs based on their career employment outcomes and specific disabilities. Vocational Rehabilitation services can include an array of services such as career counseling, academic education and training, and possibly medical and/or psychiatric treatment. In some instances,

> the VR service department might be able to provide some assistance for the student's tuition, books and supplies, adaptive technologies, or other employment related services. However, VR agencies and students are required to use maximum efforts to obtain other financial assistance. (HEATH Resource Center, 2003, p. 59)

To be eligible, students must:
- ▸ have a disability that constitutes or results in a substantial impediment to employment; and
- ▸ require VR services to prepare for, secure, retain, or regain employment. (HEATH Resource Center, 2003, p. 59)

LEARNING TO ASK THE RIGHT QUESTIONS

1. Are private scholarships or grants available specifically for students with disabilities?
2. Is a Vocational Rehabilitation liaison available on the college campus?
3. Does the financial aid office offer assistance in completing financial aid forms?
4. When are the deadlines for applying for financial aid, and how early can the financial aid application process begin?
5. Are the projected expenses at the college or university within the budget of your family?
6. What are the costs associated with attending the college or university in which you are interested (tuition, room and board, books, lab fees)?

DETERMINING CLASS SIZES

Colleges have differing class sizes dependent upon the size of the college itself. Frequently, the class sizes are larger than what most students with disabilities experience during high school. Students often find themselves sitting in classrooms with more than 50 students. In some cases, classrooms may accommodate as many as 200–300 students. Larger class sizes may make it difficult for a student with a disability to establish a place within the classroom community. If you have been receiving a great deal of support or are used to individualized instruction, you may need to select a college that offers smaller class sizes. Some universities also require instructors teaching large classes to have multiple teaching assistants. Although this information may not be easy to find on the college's Web site, you usually can find out if large classes employ teaching assistants by asking this question during a campus visit. Teaching assistants not only aid professors in classroom management, but they also often sponsor tutoring or small-group sessions to aid students in learning the class material.

Unlike the K–12 public school system, many professors do not have a mandatory attendance policy. If this is the case, students are solely responsible for managing their own attendance. Poor attendance often is less noted by professors who have larger number of students. However, some universities do implement attendance policies for all classes. If you feel that mandatory attendance will help you to remain self-motivated, you will want to look for this type of policy when researching universities.

LEARNING TO ASK THE RIGHT QUESTIONS

1. What is the average class size for courses offered in your program of study?
2. Where are classrooms located in relation to living arrangements?
3. Are teaching assistants available for courses offered in your program of study?

STUDENT DISABILITY SERVICES OFFICES

Institutions of higher learning have Student Disability Services Offices (SDSO), although they are referred to by other titles depending on the institution. SDSOs typically are located on the campus and provide a source of support for students with disabilities. When selecting a college, you should investigate the offerings that the disabilities office can provide. Some examples of services that may be available include:

- advocating for student rights;
- individual and group counseling designed for academic support for students with disabilities;
- study skills courses;
- tutors;
- counseling designed to address managing stress;
- assessment centers; and
- assistive technology resources such as magnification systems including Zoom or 20/20 Spectrum for students with visual impairments, FM systems for students with hearing impairments, Open Book or JAWS programs (voice sys-

tems that orally read the text on a computer screen), text telephones, text-to-speech software, and books on tape.

In addition to those services offered to students with disabilities, writing centers, advising centers, and reading centers may offer additional supports available to all students.

The key to maximize the supports offered through the student disability services is knowing what services are available and how to access these services. Students with disabilities are not automatically given accommodations nor will a written invitation be extended to attend counseling sessions. You must be prepared to request accommodations and to determine which service offerings you will choose to participate in or utilize. When making the decision to attend a specific college, you should consider the offerings of the disability service center in relation to your specific disability and your needs. Below are some specific considerations that can be used to evaluate the Student Disability Services Office and to determine how closely your needs are being met (Palmer, 2006).

- ► Where is the Student Disability Services Office located?
- ► Are the office personnel familiar with your specific disability?
- ► Have they served other students who have the same disability?
- ► If there is a support you need, are they able to provide it?
- ► What documentation is required for accessing the services?
- ► Do staff members receive any special training?
- ► How many office staff are employed?
- ► How are services provided through the Student Disability Services Office?
- ► What role does the Student Disability Services Office play during freshman orientation?
- ► Does the Student Disability Services Office offer training or education to faculty members regarding specific disability areas?

- ► Are faculty members required to participate in training regarding their responsibilities in working with students with disabilities?
- ► Who do parents contact if they have concerns during the school year?
- ► Does the Student Disability Services Office provide support for students who need assistance in advocating for themselves (i.e., meeting with instructors)?
- ► Are there any support groups specifically designed to meet the needs of students who have been identified with your specific disability?

Samples of some of the forms that will be required for students with disabilities to receive services through the SDSO are included in the Resources Section of this chapter.

LEARNING TO ASK THE RIGHT QUESTIONS

1. What are the levels of services offered through your university's Student Disability Services Office?
2. What is the process of obtaining accommodations through the Student Disability Services Office? How are such accommodations determined?
3. What types of assistive technology devices are available to students with disabilities?
4. What additional resources are in place for students with disabilities?
5. Are staff members provided training or do they have experience working with students with your specific disability?
6. If your specific disability directly impacts your ability to pass a required course, such as foreign language or mathematics, are course substitutions or waivers available?

VISITING COLLEGE CAMPUSES

After narrowing down college choices to two or three, it is highly recommended that you make appointments and visit the college campuses. During these visits, scheduled appointments with the

Student Disability Services Office, financial aid office, and admissions office should be held. This provides you with the opportunity to ask specific questions and to determine how well your interests and skills match the colleges and/or universities that are being considered. The campus visit also provides opportunities for students to familiarize themselves with locations of the various support systems on campus.

Most colleges and universities provide tours of the campus where writing centers, reading centers, housing facilities, academic buildings, and social areas are identified. During the campus visit, students with disabilities should take the opportunity to talk with other students currently attending the college. Students enrolled in classes will be able to share information about classes, technology usage, professors, and extracurricular involvement. The college visit provides a firsthand opportunity to determine the "feel" of the campus. It is the most effective way to become familiar with the campus environment. What attitudes toward your disability are apparent? Does the campus feel too large or small for you? How receptive do the professors seem toward students with disabilities?

Most colleges and universities provide an opportunity for a student to sit in on a class if requested. This opportunity allows a student with a disability to "personally judge the level of difficulty of the instruction, observe the interaction of the students, and gain for himself or herself a sense of relationship between the students and the faculty" (ERIC Clearinghouse on Handicapped and Gifted Children, 1989, p. 3). Sitting in on instruction also will help you to determine if you are comfortable with the class size and the various environmental factors within the classroom setting.

Prior to the campus visit you should focus on learning to ask the right questions. Advocating for oneself during the college admission process and later in life is a critical skill that students with disabilities must obtain. You should receive adequate instruction prior to interviewing at various colleges on how to actively advocate for yourself. When visiting colleges you need to able to clearly articulate your disability and how your learning differences will affect the application process. You should be prepared to state your accommodation needs in functional, real-world terms, so that postsecondary institutions will be able to effectively accommodate your needs (HEATH Resource Center, 2006).

UNDERSTANDING ADMISSION REQUIREMENTS: PREPARING TO APPLY TO COLLEGE

Universities have specific admission criteria. When selecting a college or university, the first step is to ask whether or not the college has separate admission criteria for students with disabilities. Admission criteria for institutions vary and can include:

- ► submission of SAT or ACT scores that indicate a minimum standardized score,
- ► submission of letters of recommendation,
- ► minimum GPA in secondary school education, and
- ► submission of a short essay or reflection paper.

In addition, colleges also may have a requirement for a minimum number of hours of foreign language to be completed in high school, but this is not the case in all colleges. Although there are minimum admission requirements for higher education, some colleges and universities may "consider the impact of the disability when making the admission decision" (Madaus, 2005, p. 34). However, this consideration is not required by law.

If SAT or ACT scores are required, you should review your PSAT scores (if you took it) and try to determine how you might perform on the SAT or ACT. Various computerized tutorial programs are available to assist you in preparing to take the exam. It is important to note that the assessment situation itself can be quite intimidating with a testing allocation time of approximately 4 hours. Students with specific disabilities may need—or qualify for—special accommodations during the testing period. This option is available through the submission of a Student Eligibility Form to the Students with Disabilities department of the College Board. Eligibility is based on documentation addressing seven guidelines (College Board, n.d.; see http://professionals. collegeboard.com/testing/ssd/application/guide/guidelines). Documentation must:

1. **State the specific disability**, as diagnosed (Diagnosis should be made by a person with appropriate professional credentials, should be specific, and, when appropriate, should relate the disability to the applicable professional standards. For example, DSM-IV.)
2. **Be current** (in most cases, the evaluation and diagnostic testing should have taken place within five years of the request for accommodations)
3. Provide relevant **educational, developmental, and medical history**
4. **Describe the comprehensive testing and techniques** used to arrive at the diagnosis. Include **test results with subtest scores** (standard or scaled scores) for all tests.
5. **Describe the functional limitations** (for example, the limitations to learning impacted due to the diagnosed disability)
6. Describe the **specific accommodations** being requested on College Board tests
7. Establish the **professional credentials of the evaluator** (for example, licensure; certification; area of specialization; College Board, n.d., para. 2)

If you are eligible to obtain accommodations based on the approval of the College Board, accommodations in responding, presentation, setting, and timing may be requested. Additional information, including a more thorough list of accommodations and instructions on completing and submitting the required forms, can be obtained from the College Board at http://www.collegeboard.com/disable/counsel/html/indx000.html. This Web site provides information about college admission testing for students with disabilities.

A student with a disability may struggle to meet the minimum scores required or to produce an essay that fairly represents the student's ability to be successful in the college setting. Other students may struggle with having the required GPA while attending high school. Some institutions will recognize alternative testing formats or will accept supporting documentation to show academic achievement. It is recommended that students with disabilities include supplemental information indicating why specific requirements are not met. For example, if a student does not have minimum scores on the SAT, a statement should be included that specifically addresses how the disability directly impacts the score received. Providing information about a student's disability is a voluntary act. An institution of higher education cannot require that a student disclose his or her disability.

LEARNING TO ASK THE RIGHT QUESTIONS

1. What specific standardized assessments are required for college admittance?
2. Is there a minimum expectation for scores on standardized assessments (range of acceptable scores)?
3. Are special provisions made during the application process for students with disabilities?
4. Will additional supporting materials be accepted for special review if minimum university admittance criteria are not met?
5. Do you meet the expected academic criteria determined by the university (GPA)?

CONCLUSION

Choosing a college that is right for you will affect your level of success and overall experience as a college student. You need to understand the expectations of the colleges you are interested in attending and how they match with your own personal goals. Examining your own needs and preferences in regard to academics, social opportunities, and financial needs are all important factors to consider. Taking the time to complete the Postsecondary Preference Worksheet also will help you narrow down your choices and can help direct you to the colleges that may be a better match for you. Just as important as the academic programs of a particular college is the logistical information about the college. Location, size of the college, and class size also should be considered in making your decision along with the services that are provided by the Student Disability Services Office. It is easy for students to get caught up in wanting to go to a particular college because it is a popular college among their friends, but one college is not a fit for everyone. Figure 2 shares some common pitfalls students face when making decisions about which colleges to apply to and which to attend. Take the time to research and visit the colleges you choose so that you can make the decision that is right for you.

The Resources Section of this chapter also includes some very important documents to review before attending college. The Disclosure Authorization Form, Student Intake Form, Test Form, and Disability Verification Form will provide you with sample documents to help you organize your information regarding your disability and education needs. However, it is a good idea to review these documents before you consider attending college so that you have a good idea of what gaps you will need to fill in your transition planning. These forms also can be used to aid you in compiling a dedicated place for information regarding your disability that can help you fill out applications, scholarship forms, and other documents related to college.

"I'm applying to college X because all my friends are/are not going there."

"There's only one college that's right for me."

"All colleges are the same, so why bother with all this work?"

"I'm going to college X because my father/mother/sister/brother went there (or wants me to go there)."

"College X is too expensive for me."

"I'm not applying there because I'll be rejected." (This does not mean you should avoid applying to one "long-shot" school.)

"If the one college I want doesn't want me, I'll be unhappy for the next 4 years."

Figure 2. Common pitfalls for students to avoid.

Note: From *College Planning for Gifted Students* (3rd ed., p. 92), by S. L. Berger, 2006, Waco, TX: Prufrock Press. Copyright © 2006 by Prufrock Press. Reprinted with permission.

STUDENT INTERVIEWS

What process did you use in selecting the college you wanted to attend?

James: I didn't use a specific formal process, but I did begin by thinking about what career I would be interested in. Next, I went on the Internet and researched all of the local universities within 3 hours of my parents' house that offered the degree I wanted. Because I didn't have much financial assistance, I wanted to choose a school with a high-quality education program, but reasonable costs. I narrowed it down to three different schools, including Sam Houston State University (SHSU). The reason I chose SHSU was because they offered a great education program at an extremely reasonable cost. This decision-making process was relatively easy for me, because I had been well-prepared in high school for my self-advocacy role. I was also highly motivated to make my decision.

What role did examining career goals play in the selection of Sam Houston State University?

James: The examination of career goals played a huge part in my selection of SHSU. This university is well known for being a high-quality education school and several of my teachers and administrators in public school had attended SHSU and recommended it to me. Certain schools offer more extensive programs in certain areas and part of preparing to self-advocate is to know how to identify the signs of a good program. One key point to keep in mind is that you want to avoid choosing a school based *only* on its good program. Other factors have to be considered such as the size of the campus and its rigor. The university I selected was an appropriate match for me.

What specific college options did you research?

James: Postsecondary education offers many different options for a student depending on what your needs are. Some students need a great deal of support and must attend school close to home. As much as I wanted to leave home and spread my wings, I knew that I needed to be somewhat close to my parents' house for both emotional and financial support. In many ways the idea of a community or junior college appealed to me, but on the same token I couldn't become a fully certified teacher through those institutions. I enrolled in SHSU, but I was still not sure if it was the right choice until I met the faculty in my department. One professor in particular, Dr. Simpson, was very welcoming and I couldn't wait to take classes in the special education program. This confirmed my choice and helped ease my tension about coming to a 4-year school.

What types of questions did the Student Disability Services Office answer for you?

James: They were very helpful. I scheduled my appointment with them and asked my social coach to accompany me. They answered several minor questions, but the most important questions were related to what services the office could provide. I knew what I needed in high school, but I was not sure in regard to college, because I had never experienced it before. My social coach and parents helped me come up with some ideas and questions to ask and these served as a guide in the meeting. What I've learned is that the best approach to take is to develop a list of 5 to 10 questions prior to the interview. This serves as a way to help you remember what is important and to get the most out of the meeting. In a way, this meeting serves as an interview between the institution and you to establish what they are able to do for you. In essence, you are hiring the school to support you on their campus.

Angela: The main thing I needed to know was what to do each semester to get my accommodations. I feel that the Disability Services Office pretty much answered any question I had for them.

How many colleges did you visit and what did you gain from the college campus visit?

James: After reviewing around 10 colleges and universities through the Internet and via phone, I chose 3 colleges to visit. I gained a general understanding of the college life and culture on each campus, which helped me to make informed decisions about what I liked and didn't like. Afterwards, I made a pros and cons list for each campus and compared them to each other based on 10 criteria that were important to me.

When did you determine that you had to become an advocate for yourself?

James: I made that choice during my junior year of high school when my IEP team began to discuss transition. They explained to me that I had to start making some of my own academic decisions at age 18, because I would be in charge of my IEP meetings. Again, this was a choice I had to make. My parents could no longer decide for me, even though they continued to encourage me.

Angela: There was a particular incident that occurred that made me realize that I had to become an advocate for myself. I think this realization came the day I moved into my dorm room. I realized I was on my own when my family left after moving me in my room. This was also when I had some anxieties about beginning college. I was worried about quite a few things such as being away from home, which was very hard for me at first, as well as the work load and the level of difficulty of work. I was also worried about tests because I get bad test anxiety.

How did learning to ask the right questions help you in the college planning process?

James: I didn't always know the right questions to ask. In the beginning, I relied mostly on professionals and my parents for guidance. Unfortunately, public school doesn't prepare students very well for self-advocacy. They discussed transition and what they plan to do, but they didn't actually provide much tangible resources or help in regard to asking questions.

After you determined what university you would attend, what types of anxieties did you experience, if any?

James: The most severe anxiety I felt was related to the prospect of going to a new school and being away from my parents. For the most part I was ready to go, but I think my parents were worried as well. We didn't know what to expect; we had never done this [attending college with a disability] before. The huge benefit I had was that my brother was already attending SHSU, and he had allowed me to spend the night on campus to get used to the idea. My preparation, along with my brother's support, allowed me to do well and experience a marginal level of anxiety. Preparation is the key!

Once you made the decision to attend SHSU, did you celebrate? How did you feel?

James: Absolutely, I was ecstatic. I realized that all of the years of struggling, hard work, and personal dedication were finally paying off and my dreams of being a teacher might actually happen. Despite all of the people that were cheering me on, I didn't believe I could do it until the end of my first semester at SHSU when I received my grades. I got a 4.0. I couldn't believe it. In many ways, I had begun to realize what a famous professor once said, "We cannot change the cards we are dealt, just how we play the hand." I was dealt Asperger's syndrome, what I played was victory over it.

POSTSECONDARY PREFERENCE WORKSHEET

Name of college or university: _____

Web site address: _____

Academic Characteristics	Student Comments
Highly competitive academically	
Moderately competitive	
Not competitive	
Average SAT/ACT score	
High school GPA of current freshman class	
Other	
Demographics	**Student Comments**
Size of city/town	
Size of college	
Distance from home	
Public transportation	
Parking facilities	
Access to buildings	
Food services	
Other	
Admission Policies	**Student Comments**
Minimum ACT or SAT scores	
Admission requirements	
College essay	
Specific course requirements	
Letters of teacher recommendations	
Other	
Field of Study	**Student Comments**
Availability of major	
Admission requirements for major	
Full-time years of study for completion	
Part-time years of study for completion	

Services for Students With Disabilities	Student Comments
Student Disability Services Office	
Study-skills classes	
Time-management classes	
Developmental academic classes	
Career placement services	
Note-takers	
Assistive technology	
Computer availability	
Alternative formats for course materials	
Extended time for tests	
Alternate tests administration	
Other	

Housing	Student Comments
Residence halls	
Off-campus housing	
Substance-free residence halls	
Single-gender halls	
Coed halls	
Quiet designated study hours	
Internet access in rooms/residence halls	
Cooking facilities available	
Visitation hours	
Other	

Campus Life	Student Comments
Clubs or organizations of interest	
Sports activities	
Health clinic	
Fitness center	
Counseling center	
Computer labs	
Other	

ANY UNIVERSITY
STUDENT DISABILITY SERVICES OFFICE
DISCLOSURE AUTHORIZATION FORM

Student: _____

Student ID#: _____

I authorize the Student Disability Services Office/Disability Resource Center at any university to:

❏ Exchange with   ❏ Disclose to   ❏ Obtain from

_____

Name and/or Organization Address

The following information:

❏ Psychological Evaluations   ❏ Neuropsychological Evaluations

❏ Psychological/Psychiatric Evaluations   ❏ Medical Records

❏ Other

For the following purpose(s): _____

_____

_____

_____   _____

Signature of Student   Date

_____   _____

Witness   Date

I understand that my records are protected under federal and state confidentiality laws and regulations.

ANY UNIVERSITY
STUDENT DISABILITY SERVICES OFFICE

STUDENT INTAKE FORM

Student's Name: _____

Date: _____ ID#: _____

Contact Information

Mailing Address:

Street: _____

City: _____ State: _____ Zip: _____

Permanent Address:

Street: _____

City: _____ State: _____ Zip: _____

Phone: _____ Cell: _____

E-mail: _____

Area of Study

Major: _____

Check One:

Freshman: ❏   Sophomore: ❏   Junior: ❏
Senior: ❏   Law Student: ❏   Graduate: ❏

What is your diagnosed disability?

_____

_____

_____

STUDENT INTAKE FORM, CONTINUED

Describe your disability and how it affects your performance as a student.

_____

_____

_____

List the accommodations you are requesting.

_____

_____

_____

List any accommodations that you have received in the past.

_____

_____

_____

List any assistive technology that you have used in the past.

_____

_____

_____

Is there any additional information that you would like for us to know regarding your accommodations?

_____

_____

_____

_____

_____

ANY UNIVERSITY
STUDENT DISABILITY SERVICES OFFICE
TEST FORM

Location: Student Building
DSO Testing Hours: Monday – Friday: 8:00 a.m. – 8:00 p.m.
Phone: (____)____-_____   Fax: (____)____-_____

Completed form MUST BE RETURNED TO THE DSO AT LEAST ONE WEEK prior to the date of the exam. In order to receive testing accommodation, you must have all sections completed. You may only receive the accommodations allowed and the materials allowed by your professor.

SECTION A: To be completed by the student.
All exams are to be taken during the DSO Testing Hours stated above.

Test Date: _____ Test Time: _____

Name: _____

E-mail:_____ Phone: _____

Course & Section #:_____

Instructor: _____

Accommodations needed:
❏ Extended Time:_____ ❏ Taped Format
❏ Quiet/Distraction Free Room ❏ Scribe ❏ Word Processor ❏ Reader
❏ Other: _____

_____   _____
Signature of Student   Date

Test Form, Continued

SECTION B: To be completed by the professor.

Exam Delivery (Check One):   **Exam Return (Check One):**

❏ Professor delivers to DSO   ❏ Professor picks up from DSO

❏ Professor e-mails to DSO   ❏ Student returns in sealed envelope

❏ Student delivers in sealed envelope   ❏ DSO returns: Time _____

❏ DSO picks up: Time _____

    Building _____ Room _____

Materials allowed for exam/special instructions: _____

_____

Open Book: ❏ Yes   ❏ No
Open Notes: ❏ Yes   ❏ No
Calculator: ❏ Yes   ❏ No
Dictionary: ❏ Yes   ❏ No

Additional Instructions: _____

_____

Exam Length: _____

_____
                               Professor Signature

_____   _____
Professor E-mail and Phone   Date

ANY UNIVERSITY
STUDENT DISABILITY SERVICES OFFICE
DISABILITY VERIFICATION FORM

THIS FORM IS TO BE COMPLETED BY A LICENSED PROFESSIONAL.
This student may be eligible for special accommodations at this college. In order
to provide services, we must have documentation of a disability that impairs one
or more major life functions. Please complete the form and submit to:

_____

Student Name: _____

SS#: _____

Please provide the following information in full (please be specific). This form
is not valid without a specific diagnosis and description of the disability, the
functional limitations as a result of the disability, and the signature, date, and
license number of the professional evaluator.

Disability/Diagnosis: _____

Description of assessments and methods used to make the diagnosis:

_____

_____

Description of the disability:

_____

_____

In what settings or on what academic tasks will this disability likely manifest
itself?

_____

_____

DISABILITY VERIFICATION FORM, CONTINUED

Recommendations for services and accommodations:

❏ extended time on tests   ❏ preferential seating

❏ note-taker   ❏ taped textbooks

❏ computer   ❏ tape recorder

❏ alternate testing environment   ❏ alternate testing format

❏ scribe   ❏ reader

❏ calculator   ❏ other _____

Prescribed medications, dosage, side effects:

_____

_____

I certify that all the information on this form is true and correct to the best of my knowledge.

_____   _____

Signature of Licensed Professional   Date

_____

Print Name

_____

Title or License Type and Number

_____

Contact Information

WEB SITES RELATED TO CHAPTER 3

COLLEGE BOARD: STUDENTS WITH DISABILITIES

http://professionals.collegeboard.com/testing/ssd

Considered an inside source for college admission requirements, this site provides information for students and parents to assist in simplifying planning for college.

THE ACT

http://www.actstudent.org

This site provides preparation and registration information regarding the ACT Examination. Click on the link for "Students with disabilities."

STUDENT AID ON THE WEB

https://studentaid.ed.gov

This site provides information on financial aid services and is sponsored by the federal student aid "Start Here Go Further" initiative.

THE CAREER KEY

http://www.careerkey.org

This site provides an online tool containing a career assessment that matches the student's personality with careers.

CHAPTER
FOUR

[PREPARING TO ATTEND COLLEGE]

THE APPLICATION PROCESS

ONCE you have narrowed down the list of colleges that you are interested in applying to, you will need to begin requesting applications. It typically is recommended that you apply to at least six colleges—two "reach" colleges that are more selective academically, two colleges where acceptance is likely, and two colleges where admittance is guaranteed. Some of the colleges will mail out the application forms and others may refer you to the college's Web site to download the forms. These forms take time to complete and will include some deadlines for submission. The Resources Section of this chapter includes a College Application Timeline checklist that you can use to assist you in a timely completion of your application. Counselors and college coaches are good resources to help with the application process.

WRITING THE COLLEGE ESSAY

Some colleges may require that you include a college essay or writing sample. This may seem overwhelming if you have difficulty with writing, but there is plenty of assistance to help you with this part of the application. It is important that you not shy away from applying to certain colleges just because you have to write an essay to be accepted. Remember that this is only one part of the application. Below are some helpful tips in writing a college essay.

1. Review a couple of books on college essays that can be found at most any bookstore. This will give you some insight into what the colleges may be looking for.

2. Discuss some possible topics with your English teacher. Some senior English classes work on the student's essay during the first part of the year. If not, consider using a tutor to help with the writing process or ask a teacher for help before or after school.

3. Be original! Give the admissions officers something fun to read.

4. Have someone look over your paper. Get feedback on what needs to be improved.

5. Revise and rewrite.

Also check out Figure 3, which provides insight into what colleges look for in a good essay.

REQUESTING LETTERS OF RECOMMENDATION

Another necessary part of the application will be the letters of rec-ommendation. You will need to ask at least two high school staff members, one being the school counselor and another being a teacher, and possibly an employer or close friend of the family to write a letter of recommendation. Some students also have com-munity leaders, such as the head of a nonprofit you've worked with on a regular basis or a religious group leader, to write letters of recommendation. Always remember that your recommenders should know you well—especially those who are not your teachers.

- Writing ability

- Intellectual curiosity

- Initiative and motivation

- Creativity

- Self-discipline

- Character

- Capacity for growth

- Leadership potential

- Community service

- Consistency with other elements of the student's application

Figure 3. What colleges look for in a good essay.

Note. From *College Planning for Gifted Students* (3rd ed., p. 165), by S. L. Berger, 2006, Waco, TX: Prufrock Press. Copyright © 2006 by Prufrock Press. Reprinted with permission.

Sometimes the application packet will include a form that needs to be completed by the person writing the recommendation, so you will want to make sure you have read the packet thoroughly before you complete this step. In order to assist those who will be writing the letter of recommendation, you also should type up a one-page handout that shows your GPA, organizations and club memberships, and school and community activities, as well as any other information that you would like mentioned in the letter. This ensures that the information in the letter will be a true reflection of your accomplishments. It also helps you develop a resumé for potential employment.

MAKING THE RIGHT CHOICE

Once the acceptance letters begin to arrive, you will need to begin deciding on which school is the right match for you. Unfortunately, you will probably receive a few letters that tell you that you have been wait-listed or even denied admittance, but keep in mind that most students rarely get an acceptance letter for every application they submit. It is normal to be disappointed, but it is important that you do not take it personally. The college may have had an unusually large amount of applicants, or they may have had only a specific number of spaces available. Even so, you need to feel proud that you put forth the effort to apply to a variety of colleges. By doing so, you gave yourself some choice in choosing the college that is the right fit for you.

On a rare occasion, a student may not be accepted to any of the colleges to which he or she applies. If this happens to you, the next step would be to apply to a community college for the first 2 years of study and then transfer to a 4-year college once you have proven yourself as a capable student. The transfer process often is more cost effective and still allows you to achieve the same end goals.

LEARNING TO ASK THE RIGHT QUESTIONS

1. Have you chosen the colleges to which you want to apply?
2. Have you requested an application packet from each of those colleges?
3. Have you reviewed the College Application Timeline checklist, so you can meet all of the deadlines?
4. Have you written your college essay?
5. Have you asked teachers, employers, and friends to write a letter of recommendation?
6. Have you prepared your one-page handout to assist the persons writing the letters of recommendation?
7. Have you chosen the college that you will attend?

DISABILITY SERVICE COORDINATOR

One of the main differences between college and high school is that in the college setting the student is responsible for initiating or beginning the process of requesting accommodations for coursework. After being accepted into the college of your choice, you should determine if you will disclose information regarding your disability to the university. Some students with disabilities feel that they can successfully experience college life without the use of additional supports and services. However, most students with disabilities find it beneficial to disclose their disability to the Disability Service Coordinator and begin to lay the foundation for receiving support services. Professors on college campuses see many students enter into programs without disclosing their disability. Some of these students struggle with the day-to-day responsibilities of time management. The decision to self-disclose is a personal one. Great consideration to this decision should be given, and ultimately the decision should be left to you.

A critical question that you should ask yourself when determining whether or not to disclose your disability is, "Will I benefit from attending a university or college without academic accommodations?" If you find that you will not receive a direct benefit from attending postsecondary education without accommodations, then you should consider the following questions as well:

1. How significant is the disability?
2. How much does the nature or manifestation of the disability conflict with the needs of the educational program?
3. How open is the educational program to recognizing and accommodating individuals with disabilities? (HEATH Resource Center, 2003, p. 107)

It is imperative that a student understands that if he chooses not to disclose his disability then the institution will not be accountable for providing academic accommodations or supports. If the student determines that he or she will disclose his disability, then the next step would be to begin the process. To initiate this process, you should begin by setting up an appointment to visit with the Disability Service Coordinator. The Disability Service Coordinator will assist you in understanding the process in which you will have to take part in order to receive accommodations and other services specifically related to your disability. If you do not contact the Disability Service Coordinator and provide the required documentation, you will not receive accommodations. In addition, you should be sure to ask how often an application for accommodations needs to be filed. Is it per semester, term, or academic year?

The Disability Service Coordinator will need you to be prepared to present the required documentation forms. Most colleges and universities request information such as your high school IEP and most recent comprehensive evaluation. This may include the diagnostic report for your disability, which can be obtained from your school psychologist, educational diagnostician, or medical doctor. If your most recent assessment is older than 3 years, the college or university may request that additional testing be done to determine whether or not you will be eligible for accommodations in the college setting. Some universities offer counseling centers where the assessment can be done for an additional fee. After reviewing the required documentation forms, the Disability Service Coordinator will work with you to determine which accommodations are needed. It is important to remember that the law does not require that all accommodations given in high school also be offered in the college or university setting. You should be prepared to explain how your specific disability impacts your learning and which accommodations will assist you in becoming more academically successful. Chapter 5 focuses on accommodations and academic success.

Virginia's College Guide for Students with Disabilities (Virginia Department of Education, 2003) recommends that students practice responding to the following questions prior to their meeting with the Disability Service Coordinator:

- ▸ Can you describe your educational background?
- ▸ Can you describe your disability?

- What are your strengths and weaknesses, in and outside the classroom?
- What adaptive equipment are you currently using?
- What training did you receive in using this adaptive equipment?
- Who provided your technical support?
- How did you communicate with your instructors about using your adaptive equipment in the classroom? How did they respond?
- What appropriate academic adjustments and auxiliary aids and services do you have to assist you for class?
- Explain how your accommodations have made you successful. (p. 32)

Being able to respond to the questions above will assist the Disability Service Coordinator in making recommendations for services and accommodations that are best matched to your individual needs.

LEARNING TO ASK THE RIGHT QUESTIONS

1. Where is the Student Disability Services Office located?
2. Who is the Disability Service Coordinator that you will be meeting with?
3. How soon can an appointment be scheduled to meet with the Disability Service Coordinator?
4. Do you have all of the necessary forms that will be needed to document your disability? Are they all located in one easy-to-find place?
5. Are you prepared to answer the questions above in an effort to advocate for yourself?

RELEASE OF INFORMATION

At the time of the meeting, students with disabilities will find that the role of the parent differs from the role he or she played during high school. Parents are limited in their ability to communicate with the college or university without the written consent of the student.

This is a voluntary act, but for some students it may be necessary to give written consent for your parents to be able to communicate with the college or university. Depending on the specific disability that you have, you may find it difficult to communicate effectively about financial matters, accommodations, safety concerns, and other college-related issues. Thus, this may be information that your parents could effectively communicate or advocate for on your behalf.

Many students with disabilities sign a "release of information" so that the university or college can legally communicate with the student's parents regarding progress (including student grades). Throughout the high school years, many parents are very active in the planning of their child's IEP. In postsecondary education, as the student, you are responsible for making sure that you are following the correct degree plans and making necessary payments to the college and university. Handling such matters may be overwhelming for someone with limited self-advocacy skills.

LEARNING TO ASK THE RIGHT QUESTIONS

1. Is a standard form available to request a release of information?
2. What information can be shared with the identified person listed on the release form?
3. Are you prepared to advocate for yourself in regard to financial and academic matters if a release of information form is not signed?
4. Do you have the time management and organization skills needed to maintain designated timelines for tuition payments and eligibility timelines?

FRESHMAN ORIENTATION PROGRAMS

Prior to the start of the semester, students will be provided with information on their university's freshman orientation. Some colleges have orientation earlier in the summer, but for many colleges it is a few days prior to the beginning of the fall semester. This gives you and your parents a little extra time to familiarize yourselves with your new living and academic environment. At many universities, students also will be given a resource packet that will include information regarding all aspects of university life and academic life (more generic information on university life can be found in Chapter 7).

For a student with a disability, freshman orientation provides the opportunity to reduce anxiety, obtain valuable information about student services, orient him or her with the university campus, and begin to develop friendships with other new students. The Student Disability Services Office may offer an additional orientation for students with disabilities in which more in-depth service support information is shared. Regardless of the orientation that students attend, the experience is extremely meaningful for students with disabilities. We highly recommend attending a freshman orientation session.

Often freshman orientation (possibly called a freshman weekend or camp) involves an overnight stay on the campus before the school year starts. Freshman weekends typically involve students staying at one of the campus dormitories. For students with a specific disability, this overnight stay provides a glimpse of what dorm life and/or independent living is like. Resident Assistants (RAs) are typically involved in the dormitory experience. Making contact with the designated RA that will be living in your dorm will allow you to communicate your needs with the RA prior to the first official moving day.

Another positive aspect of the freshman orientation experience is utilizing time after the campus tour to seek out where specific classes are held. Orientation staff typically is available to assist students in finding classrooms and performing "trial runs" of their schedule. Most students, regardless of whether or not they have a disability, express concerns about getting lost on campus or arriving late to class. This dry run will allow you to be more comfortable with traveling across campus.

In addition to having the opportunity to discuss living arrangements with the RA, students often are provided with preplanned social activities. The social activities are designed to facilitate opportunities for students to meet each other and develop friendships, as well as experience university life and create school spirit. These activities are great ways to meet other incoming students without the pressure of the first days of school. At several campuses, students involved with student government or student activities attend the events and offer insight on the day-to-day college experience. We encourage students to take advantage of all of the activities they feel comfortable attending—this experience can go a long way toward preparing you to start your university career.

LEARNING TO ASK THE RIGHT QUESTIONS

1. Have you read all of the information regarding your university's freshman orientation?
2. Do you know what paperwork you will need to bring to orientation and what personal belongings will be needed?
3. If an overnight stay is required for freshman orientation, are private rooms available or needed?
4. Is a separate parents' orientation offered?
5. Will the Student Disability Services Office offer a special orientation for students with disabilities?

HOUSING ACCOMMODATIONS

Although deciding where to live can be both exciting and challenging, many considerations have to be made in making the best possible choice for you. College success depends on attending classes and fulfilling the requirements of each course. If you have a physical disability that requires additional time to get from place to place, it may be more practical for you to live on campus close to the academic buildings, dining hall, library, computer lab, and other necessary facilities. If you have decided to live at home, you will want to research transportation options. One consideration is where parking is located or if shuttle services are available from the dormitory or apartment to the location of where your program of study is offered. If you will be walking to class, you will want to check on the distance you will need to walk and determine if you are physically able to handle the length of the walk.

When considering housing arrangements, keep in mind that the place one lives extends beyond the place he sleeps. Selecting to live in the dormitory poses benefits, as well as risks, for a student with a disability. Frequently, dormitory settings have unspoken rules regarding social interaction among students living in the same building and sharing facilities. For some disability areas, this can be a challenge.

Other challenges that may be encountered are the lack of structured quiet times or study hours. Some colleges and university housing facilities offer study rooms or study halls in which the expectations revolve around a quieter environment during a specified time period. In addition to studying, students may need to overcome the need for privacy when taking care of hygiene. Dorm settings may be designed with communal restroom facilities. This means that all students on a floor or in a block of rooms are expected to shower in restrooms allocated on each floor. However, some dorms offer suites or private restroom facilities.

If you are living on campus, you may find that additional housing accommodations may be required. If additional accommodations are needed, you should contact the Disability Service Coordinator to make the request for the accommodations.

Additional accommodations that the university or college may be able to provide are wheelchair accessible bathtubs and rooms (for students with orthopedic impairments), Braille numbering (for students with visual impairments), and/or strobe lighting (for students with hearing impairments).

Another issue that tends to be overlooked is the need for laundry facilities. Students often have their laundering needs met at home during the elementary and high school years. If this has been the case, learning to and knowing how to operate coin-operated laundry machines should be taken care of prior to attendance at college. Most apartments either have washers and dryers in the apartment or, like dorms, have designated laundry facilities for the entire community to share.

A Housing Checklist can be found in the Resources Section of this chapter to collect and keep records of the housing accommodations for each institution. There also is enough space in the "Yes" column for additional notes. Using this type of checklist will help narrow your choices and assist you in the decision-making process regarding college housing options.

LEARNING TO ASK THE RIGHT QUESTIONS

1. How far from campus are the living facilities located and are you able to manage the distance needed to walk to campus?
2. If shuttles are used at the campus, where are shuttle pick-up stops located and where can you get a copy of the shuttle schedule? Are there fees associated with this service?
3. If you choose to live off campus and have to drive to campus, is parking available near the buildings in which you will be attending class?
4. Do the facilities in which you choose to live have a location in which "study rules" apply (separate room or designated floor)?
5. If living in a dorm, are female and male students housed separately? Are there restrictions on visitation hours and curfews?
6. Does a resident advisor live in the building and, if so, how is he or she accessed? What is his or her designated role within the building?
7. Are computers, TVs, or cable available for students?

CHOOSING A ROOMMATE

Choosing a roommate can be a difficult process. Most college housing departments give incoming freshman a questionnaire to match them to compatible roommates. Some of these questionnaires will ask general questions about your living and study habits, although others are very detailed and specific. Either way, it is important to answer all questions honestly. In other words, *you* need to complete the form. Parents and teachers may know some things about the student's living and study habits, but they probably do not know everything. Schools typically will try to match up lifestyles, so the more information they have, the better the chances that you will be placed with someone who is compatible with you. Issues dealing with neatness, sleeping habits, and noise level may seem minor, but they can make a big difference in a successful college experience. An example of a roommate questionnaire can be found at the end of this chapter in the Resources Section. You also may choose to select your roommate from a friend, classmate, or family member already attending or also entering the college. This can provide a level of comfort an unknown roommate does not. However, many of the same ideas about compatibility still apply.

For a student with a disability such as Asperger's syndrome, he or she may struggle with the social interactions that occur when sharing a dormitory room with another individual. Some students prefer to have a single occupancy room. When applying for housing the housing department needs to be informed of this request if this is your preference. Students with disabilities should be prepared to provide documentation that supports the need for a single occupancy room (social and sensory issues should be addressed in the documentation). If single occupancy rooms are available, they may have an additional fee attached to them.

Other students with disabilities find that dormitory living, even if a single occupancy room is available, does not meet their individual needs. Living off campus in an apartment also is an option that can be examined. This provides you with the opportunity to socialize according to your own timeframe. You also will have the opportunity to avoid social expectations often encountered in a dormitory setting. However, you will be expected to take care of responsibilities such as paying rent and bills on time that are covered in your single fee for dormitory living. With many of the other choices you will have to make about your college experience, the various housing options must be weighed carefully.

LEARNING TO ASK THE RIGHT QUESTIONS

1. Is the roommate I am selecting socially compatible with me (cleanliness, study habits, waking and bed times, etc.)?
2. Are single occupancy rooms available if a roommate situation is not appropriate? If so, what are the fees associated with this and what is the process for requesting single occupancy rooms?

CONCLUSION

Narrowing down your choices is only the first step in getting into the college of your choice. The next step is the application process, and it is going to take a lot of work and commitment on your part to make sure the application is complete and submitted on time. Using the College Application Timeline as a checklist to keep you on track will ensure that you meet all required deadlines. Once you have been accepted and chosen the college you will attend, you will have to decide on whether or not to disclose your disability. Most students find it beneficial to disclose their disability so that they can receive the academic supports they will need to be able to perform up to their academic potential. The sooner you contact the Student Disability Services Office, the more prepared they will be to make sure you receive the requested accommodations.

Another critical decision that has to be made at this point involves your housing arrangements. The college typically will have you complete a questionnaire about yourself, so that it can match you up with another student who has similar interests. It is important to be honest when completing the questionnaire, but it is your decision if, when, and how to disclose your disability to your roommate. Just remember, honesty is probably the best policy in being able to live together and accommodate each other's differences in regard to personality, learning styles, and habits.

STUDENT INTERVIEWS

How did you decide on your living arrangements for college?

James: With much difficulty, we debated the pros and cons of having and not having a roommate. Fortunately, I had an option that represented an in-between for me. My brother Greg was living in a house that had extra unused bedrooms and by rooming with him, I was getting a roommate, but it was one I knew very well. Now that I look back at that decision, I feel we made the right choice. When I was first starting college, the last thing we wanted was for an issue like a roommate to become a problem and because of our choice, it didn't. It allowed me to focus on classes and my living skills without the pressure of a new person.

Angela: I lived in a dorm the first year and then an apartment the rest of the time. The first 2 years I did not choose my roommates and then after that I started rooming with people I had met while in classes. My dorm roommate was the best roommate placement ever and we have become great friends. Even though I'm pretty easy going and easy to get along with, the roommates I thought would be great ended up not working out. However, I do think it is a great idea to room with someone of similar interests and majors.

What factors did you consider in choosing a roommate?

James: Because I really didn't have one, except for my brother, this is a tough question. However, I did think about this in case the situation didn't work out. My biggest concerns were shared bathrooms, social life, and cleanliness. I didn't want a really messy roommate or one that held a party at our place every other night. In addition, the idea of sharing a bathroom was scary because I have very particular grooming rituals and a resistance to changes in my schedule. This is an area to which all college students should give careful consideration.

Did you disclose your disability to your roommate?

Angela: Once I got to know my roommate I informed her of my disability just by explaining what it was and what I have problems with along with examples of what it is like to deal with these issues.

What suggestions would you have for students who are trying to decide on living arrangements, including decisions on roommates?

James: I would suggest four things . . .

1. Be open to the idea of a roommate, given you can reach some compromises.
2. Don't be afraid to communicate your needs and concerns because you have to live there for a year, and you don't want to feel uncomfortable in your own home.
3. Try to resolve any disagreements with your roommate first before going to your parents or your school because if you leave him out, he will feel like you didn't give him a chance.
4. Look at all living options, both on campus and off, because often off-campus living is more adjustable and they tend to work with you more because you are seen as a customer. Also,

off-campus living is not always more expensive, but on the same token it is not always as nice.

Do you have any helpful tips for living with a roommate?

James: In addition to what I shared above, I would encourage being honest and open with your roommate about your needs and your disability. He may be much more willing to accommodate you if you are honest and relaxed. Despite the issues that occur with roommates, some of the best college friendships happen because of your living arrangements, so don't feel like you have to be a stranger; you may have a lot in common. Remember that half of your college education is not in your classrooms, but in your social life and the friendships that you make.

Angela: I think that even if you do choose your roommates, they don't always turn out like you think they would. Regardless of whom you live with, you have to make the best of it and understand that everyone is different.

COLLEGE APPLICATION TIMELINE

Use this timeline to help keep track of the application process. Check off each item once it is completed.

SEPTEMBER

- ❏ Choose the colleges that you would like to attend.
- ❏ Request application packets.
- ❏ Request a copy of your high school transcript.
- ❏ Type up a one-page handout that shows your GPA; organizations and club memberships; school and community activities; and any other information that may be helpful for those persons writing the letters of recommendation.

OCTOBER

- ❏ Begin filling out the college applications.
- ❏ Mark the deadline for each college application on your calendar.
- ❏ Ask for letters of recommendation from two high school staff members, and possibly an employer or family friend.
- ❏ Take the SAT or ACT again if you want to improve your previous scores.
- ❏ Complete the college essay or writing sample.
- ❏ Research possible scholarships and financial aid.

NOVEMBER–DECEMBER

- ❏ Submit college applications before the deadline.
- ❏ Continue to research possible scholarships.

JANUARY

- ❏ Complete and submit the Free Application for Federal Student Aid (FAFSA) by mail or online starting January 1 if you are interested in receiving financial assistance.

FEBRUARY–MARCH

❏ If you have not received notification of receipt, contact the colleges to confirm that they received your application.

APRIL–MAY

❏ Based on your acceptance and rejection or wait-list letters, make your decision about which college you want to attend.

❏ Submit required paperwork and deposits to confirm that you are accepting their offer. You may include your documentation required by the Student Disability Services Office if you are seeking accommodations or you may schedule an appointment to meet with them.

❏ Visit the college where you will be attending.

HOUSING CHECKLIST

University:

Are the following options available? If yes, is there anything I should remember about the options that could help in the decision-making process?

Residence halls	❑ No	❑ Yes
Ease of accessibility	❑ No	❑ Yes
Tobacco- and alcohol-free residence halls	❑ No	❑ Yes
Single-occupancy rooms	❑ No	❑ Yes
Coed halls	❑ No	❑ Yes
Male only/female only halls	❑ No	❑ Yes
Visitation hours	❑ No	❑ Yes
Internet access in rooms	❑ No	❑ Yes
Study areas in residence halls	❑ No	❑ Yes
Quiet hours in residence halls	❑ No	❑ Yes
Computers in residence halls	❑ No	❑ Yes
Cooking facilities available	❑ No	❑ Yes
Dining facilities/accessibility	❑ No	❑ Yes
Off-campus housing/costs	❑ No	❑ Yes
Accessibility of commute to campus	❑ No	❑ Yes
Parking for student	❑ No	❑ Yes
Public transportation	❑ No	❑ Yes

SAMPLE ROOMMATE QUESTIONNAIRE

This form is designed to help our office match you with a roommate. Please answer the questions as accurately as possible. If there is someone in particular with whom you would like to room, please include his or her name on this form. Roommate assignments will be made on July 1. We will do our best to fill your request.

PLEASE TYPE OR PRINT.

Name: _____ Male ❑   Female ❑

Street: _____

City: _____ State: _____ Zip: _____

Phone: _____ Cell: _____

Current E-mail Address: _____

Do you already have someone you would like to room with? ❑ Yes ❑ No

If yes, please give his or her name and contact information. _____

_____

TELL US ABOUT YOU.

MUSIC

What type of music do you listen to? _____

_____

Do you listen to music when studying/in your room? (check all that apply)
❑ yes ❑ no ❑ sometimes ❑ loud ❑ soft ❑ medium ❑ I use headphones

Do you mind your roommate listening to music when studying/in your room? (check all that apply)
❑ yes ❑ no ❑ sometimes ❑ loud ❑ soft ❑ medium ❑ He/she needs to wear headphones

NEATNESS

Please **choose one** of the following to describe yourself:

❏ clean ❏ a little messy ❏ extremely messy

What should your roommate know about your view of keeping a room clean?

_____

_____

PERSONALITY

Please **choose one** of the following to best describe yourself:

❏ outgoing ❏ a little outgoing ❏ reserved

Please **choose one** of the following to describe your ideal roommate:

❏ outgoing ❏ a little outgoing ❏ reserved ❏ it doesn't matter

What are your hobbies/interests? _____

_____

_____

BEDTIME AND WAKE-UP

I like to stay up late. ❏ yes ❏ no If yes, how late? _____

Does it depend on your class schedule? Explain. _____

_____

_____

I am generally: ❏ a light sleeper ❏ heavy sleeper

Any sleeping habits we should know about? _____

_____

_____

Study Habits

Do you think you will study in your room? (check one)

❏ yes   ❏ no   ❏ maybe

If yes, what times do you think you will study in your room?
(check all that apply)

❏ early mornings   ❏ weekday afternoons   ❏ weekday evenings
❏ late at night   ❏ weekends

Do you anticipate studying in your room with others? (check one)

❏ yes   ❏ no   ❏ maybe

Dorm Life

Please check which statement best describes your thoughts about dorm life.
(check one)

❏ I want to have a room where everyone wants to hang out!

❏ I want to have a room where friends come by occasionally.

❏ I don't want other people spending time in my room.

**Roommate changes or requests can be made after the first three weeks of
the semester, but we cannot guarantee a room or roommate change.**

WEB SITES RELATED TO CHAPTER 4

WHAT TO DO IF YOU'RE WAIT-LISTED
http://www.collegeboard.com/student/apply/letters-are-in/124.html
Information is provided that will assist students in knowing what steps to take if they have been put on a college's wait list.

LEARNING DISABILITY: AT COLLEGE AND WORK
http://www.ncld.org/content/view/382/339
The site provides a guide to help manage a learning disability in the various areas of life.

POST ITT–DISABILITY SERVICES
http://www.postitt.org/disability_services/index.shtml
This site provides information about the Disability Service Offices that are found on college campuses and discusses their role in providing academic supports to students with disabilities.

EDUCATION QUEST
http://www.educationquest.org/writingtips.asp
This site provides tips for writing a successful college entrance essay.

CHAPTER
FIVE

ᴀᴄᴀᴅᴇᴍɪᴄꜱ

ADVOCATING FOR ACADEMIC SUCCESS

Sɪɴᴄᴇ the early 1990s when IDEA mandated increased student involvement in transition planning, promoting self-determination has been recognized as a best practice in the education of students with disabilities (Chambers et al., 2007). Self-determination is defined as a combination of skills, knowledge, and beliefs that enables a person to engage in goal-directed, self-regulated, autonomous behavior. An understanding of your strengths and limitations, together with a belief in yourself as a capable and effective learner, are essential to your self-determination and have a positive influence on improving your academic performance (Field et al., 1998).

Students who are self-determined are more likely to succeed at the college level, because they know what they want and how to get it. Hopefully, training in self-determination will begin during your public school years, so that you are better prepared to advocate for your own needs at the college level. Once the semester begins, it is your sole responsibility to advocate for your needs both in and out of the classroom with the assistance of the Disability Service Coordinator. So, how does this responsibility apply to the classroom?

For each of your courses, it is your responsibility to disclose your disability to the instructor. This typically includes providing the instructor with written documentation from the Disability Service Coordinator that confirms your disability and identifies the list of approved accommodations. You may want to schedule a brief meeting with your instructors to discuss the accommodations that have been approved by the university.

Most instructors know that students with disabilities are protected under the law; however, they may not have the full knowledge of what that law entails. Nonetheless, college-level instructors are expected to possess the skills to provide instructional accommodations for students with disabilities (Eckes & Ochoa, 2005).

ACADEMIC ADVISING

Adjusting to the college environment is full of new challenges for all students, but for students with disabilities, the responsibility of managing academic coursework along with accommodations presents a unique set of challenges (Getzel & Thoma, 2008). Understanding and knowing what is required to meet your own academic and personal needs is the first step to a successful college experience. As stated earlier, this process begins at freshman orientation when the student typically has a scheduled meeting with their preassigned academic advisor. It is the advisor's role to assist the student in planning his or her academic program. Often, this same advisor will assist you throughout your academic career.

In order to make the most of the initial meeting with the academic advisor, you will want to be familiar with the academic program you have chosen to pursue. Becoming familiar with the Web site and the university catalogue also will help you prepare questions that will need to be answered by the academic advisor.

LEARNING TO ASK THE RIGHT QUESTIONS

1. Are you familiar with the university's Web site, and specifically, the information that discusses the program in which you are interested?
2. Do you have a copy of the university catalogue?
3. Do you know what paperwork you will need to bring for the meeting with your academic advisor?
4. Do you have a list of questions for your academic advisor?

CHOOSING COURSES

Although the college experience can seem overwhelming for students with learning disabilities, adapting the traditional pacing for a course of study has proved to be an effective programming variable (McGuire & Shaw, 1987). A student taking two or three courses may be successful, but may not be able to handle a full course load. Many instructors expect students to spend at least one hour outside of class for every hour spent in class. That means a student taking 12 credit hours would spend at least 36 hours each week completing assignments and preparing for class. Even with accommodations, a student with a disability may need more time to complete assignments. Therefore, you may want to consider a reduced course load. If you choose to take a reduced load and you are on financial aid, examine the financial aid criteria closely. Some forms of financial aid are dependent on the student taking 12 semester hours. This typically is considered the number of hours for an undergraduate student to be considered a full-time student.

Colleges and universities are not required to alter admissions requirements or make any changes to the program requirements for students with disabilities once they have been admitted. You should not assume that the college will waive or substitute certain courses once you are admitted. You can make requests, but it is up to the academic committee to make that decision. If the committee decides that another course will meet the requirements of your degree plan, they may be willing to make the substitution or waiver. However, keep in mind that postsecondary institutions are not going to make any changes to a student's academic program that would lower the university's academic standards (LDOnline, 2008).

If you have made the decision to disclose your disability to the university in order to receive accommodations, you may want to discuss this information with your academic advisor, as well, especially if the college has approved a reduced course load. This information may influence the way the advisor designs your course of study.

In addition, your parents will need to check with their insurance companies about course load requirements. Most insurance companies continue to cover full-time college students who are on their parents' insurance policy, but it is the decision of the insurance company to define what they consider to be a full-time student.

When deciding on how many courses a student can successfully complete in one semester, the student needs to be aware of some of the differences in the academic environment between high school and college. The following is a list of differences between high school and college provided by WNY Collegiate Consortium and Disability Advocates that need to be considered when you are developing your course of study. The differences include (WNY, n.d.):

- less contact with instructors,
- less individual feedback,
- more academic competition from peers,
- more class lecture time,
- independent reading assignments required more often,
- classes meet less often and for fewer hours,
- courses last 16 weeks or less,
- effective library skills are needed,
- more emphasis is placed on understanding theory,

- courses may be offered online or by videotape,
- harder work is required for an A or B,
- semester grades may be based on just two or three test scores,
- more major writing assignments are given, and
- essay exams are more common.

It is essential that you understand yourself as a learner when planning your course of study. You may want to refer to the Self-Advocacy Skills Worksheet you completed in Chapter 2 to assist you in choosing courses and making decisions about the course load.

LEARNING TO ASK THE RIGHT QUESTIONS

1. How many courses can you successfully complete in a semester?
2. How much content can you read between class meetings? (Keep in mind that most courses meet every other day.)
3. How much writing can you complete between class meetings?
4. Do you have effective library skills?
5. Do you know how to use the Internet for research purposes?
6. Do you know how to use a word processing program to complete papers and other projects?

SCHEDULING

Will you be able to wake up and pay attention in an 8 a.m. class? This is an important consideration for all college students—especially those who have difficulties managing their time (see the discussion on time management). In addition, some students with disabilities may be on medication that makes it difficult for them to attend an early morning class. Therefore, it may be better to schedule classes later in the day. The number of sections offered for a particular course will depend on the number of students needing to complete the course as part of their program of study.

Therefore, you may not always have a lot of options in scheduling courses. Many instructors may not take attendance, but you will still be held responsible for learning the information covered during each class and for completing assignments, projects, and exams on time.

In some cases, if a course is not offered at a time that is most beneficial to your learning or if a course fills up before you can register for it, you may want to put off taking the course until the next semester and replace it with another course needed to complete your degree plan. This is something you will want to discuss with your academic advisor, but you should keep in mind that there is some flexibility in the order in which you complete the courses required to graduate.

COURSE REQUIREMENTS

Most instructors give a copy of the course syllabus to students on the first day of class, or they may even post it online prior to the first class meeting. As soon as you get the syllabus, it is important that you review the document and make a list of any questions you may have about the course. Some of these may include questions about the class format, class requirements such as amount of reading and writing, types of exams given, and the instructor's teaching style. You may want to schedule a brief meeting with the instructor after the first class so the instructor can address these questions early in the semester. This is an effective way to minimize the stress and misunderstandings that may occur between you and your instructor in regard to course requirements. You also may use this same meeting to disclose your disability, turn in a copy of the documentation to the instructor, and discuss how the accommodations will be implemented within that particular course.

The syllabus typically includes information about the required texts for the course. You can purchase textbooks a couple of weeks before the class begins, so you have a chance to read through some of the information you will be learning. Some students take advantage of this by reading slightly ahead of the course syllabus, starting in the summer, which allows you a little more time for reading between class meetings. Several university bookstores offer the opportunity for students to preorder books by entering their class schedules. This process is called by different names across universities. However, the process is similar at most universities. A student can order the textbooks based off his or her schedule, usually using an online program the bookstore has created. The schedule is accessed by the university bookstore, the instructors' booklists are checked, and the correct books are pulled, bagged, and ready for pick-up by the student. In most cases, you can specify if you want new or used books. All you have to do is go to the bookstore and pay for the books. This saves a lot of time and assures that you are purchasing the correct books. Keep in mind that some professors will ask for supplementary textbooks that are optional. You can wait to purchase these books until you receive additional information from your instructor. Preordering books is a great option for first-semester students, but you also should familiarize yourself with how the bookstore works so that you can pick up any materials (like those supplementary textbooks) later. One downside to preordering books is that some campuses have multiple bookstores, and some students prefer to shop around the stores for the best pricing and conditions of used books. But, for your first semester, preordering books is an excellent way to ensure you have what you need, when you need it.

Also, you can use the syllabus to develop a calendar plan for completing assignments and projects. You should carefully review the syllabus for any information that requires the use of specialized equipment or technology. For example, many universities utilize Web-based programs integrated into instruction such as Blackboard or WebCT. These programs allow professors to post readings, assignment sheets, and syllabi. They also allow professors to collect student work submitted via the Web. If you are not familiar with these programs, you can participate in university-wide training sessions. Many institutions offer technology training sessions early in the semester and prior to the beginning of courses. Often these training sessions are conducted by university libraries, which teach library-specific technology, such as the use of the school catalog and Internet databases, along with training on basic computer programs. However, with the increased use of technology, you should be well-versed in using software programs such as Microsoft Word, PowerPoint, and Excel. These programs are likely to be utilized quite often by your instructors. Course instructors typically do not provide training on software programs unless they are directly related to the course offering.

PREPARING ACADEMICALLY

As previously mentioned, the role of the student drastically changes when moving from the high school setting to the college campus. This is particularly true with academic responsibilities. Although specific accommodations can be granted to students with disabilities (further information on accommodations in the classroom is shared below), the university is not required to prepare students or to strengthen skills necessary to reduce the intensification of the academic workload. You should examine areas in which you can strengthen your own academic skills. Getzel and Wehman (2005) provided examples of areas for strengthening academic skills. These particular skills can be addressed through attendance at workshops, during secondary education, or in the home environment prior to attending college. Most college campuses will offer mini-workshops or seminars to the general population of students to address the following areas:

- ► writing strategies,
- ► reading skills,
- ► proofreading skills,
- ► color-coding information and other organization skills,
- ► mnemonics for memorization,
- ► test-taking strategies,
- ► managing time,
- ► videotaping for self-evaluation,
- ► role-playing exam questions or presentations, and
- ► general study skills (additional information can be obtained in the next section).

You should contact the Student Disability Services Office for information regarding dates and offerings of any seminars and workshops offered on your campus. In addition, you should receive some instruction prior to entering college on those skills necessary to use a computer and/or specific assistive technology that you may be using or accessing through the Disability Services Office.

EFFECTIVE USE OF STUDY SKILLS

Knowing how to use study skills benefits all students, but for students with disabilities, the use of effective study skills is crucial in successfully completing an academic program. You will want to develop strategies to assist you in learning information that is presented in a variety of formats that may be different from your high school classes. You need to understand your own learning style even though college classes are not always taught in the same way that students learn. You can refer to the Study Skills Checklist at the end of this chapter to help identify how you learn information.

When you understand how you learn and retain new information, you will be more successful in developing study skills that match your own learning style. Also, time management in this digital world can be very challenging, but learning to manage your own time lowers stress, while procrastination increases stress. The following is a list of tips you can use to not only manage your academic classes but in managing your time as you prepare for class.

TIPS FOR COMPLETING READING ASSIGNMENTS

- ► Before the first class, buy the textbook.
- ► Scan the first chapter and look at the pictures, graphs, and headings.
- ► Write down unknown vocabulary words and look them up.
- ► Use Post-It® notes to identify key words or sections.
- ► Highlight important information in the chapter.
- ► Read in short time blocks.
- ► Keep up with assigned readings.

TIPS FOR COMPLETING WRITTEN ASSIGNMENTS

- ► Brainstorm ideas for your topic.
- ► Research your topic using the library's online databases.
- ► Use graphic organizers to help organize your thoughts and plan out your paper or response to an assignment. (See http://www.unl.edu/csi/wcomp.html for sample organizers.)
- ► Use index cards to help organize the information.
- ► Go to the writing center for help (available at most colleges).

TIPS FOR NOTE-TAKING

- ► Be prepared—have the necessary materials to take notes.
- ► Consider having a spiral notebook for each course so all notes can be kept together.

- Use short phrases instead of complete sentences.
- Ask questions for clarification.
- Use abbreviations to reduce the amount of writing.
- Compare your notes with another student in class.
- Use a tape recorder. You will need to obtain the consent of the instructor unless it is in your approved accommodations.
- Get a copy of the instructor's notes. This may be in your approved accommodations.
- Use specific note-taking strategies. (See http://www.unl.edu/csi/notes.html for examples.)

TIPS FOR ORGANIZATION

- Keep an organized notebook for each course that includes the course syllabus and any guidelines or rubrics for assignments.
- Use color-coded folders to organize classwork and assignments.
- Reduce excess materials in and on your desk.
- Label spaces.

TIPS FOR TIME MANAGEMENT

- Purchase a weekly planner/calendar.
- Record assignments, due dates, and exam schedules in your planner.
- Schedule study times/reading sessions/project work on a daily basis.
- Divide assignments into smaller sections and set a due date for each section.
- Choose a location that is conducive to studying.

LEARNING TO ASK THE RIGHT QUESTIONS

1. Have you completed the Study Skills Checklist in the Resources Section of this chapter?
2. Do you have a weekly planner/calendar?
3. Do you have strategies in place to help you complete reading and writing assignments?
4. Do you have a note-taking system?

ACCOMMODATIONS IN THE CLASSROOM

Under Section 504 of the Rehabilitation Act, institutions are required to make modifications in academic requirements as necessary to ensure that such requirements do not discriminate or have the effect of discriminating against a qualified applicant with handicaps (Sec. 104.44a). Based on this statement, reasonable accommodations are to be provided on a case-by-case basis dependent on the student's documentation. Academic accommodations have been defined as "practices and procedures in the areas of presentation, response, setting, and timing/scheduling that provide equitable access during instruction and assessment for students with disabilities" (Thompson, Morse, Sharpe, & Hall, 2005, p. 17), but the responsibility of attaining accommodations in college is a two-way street (Scott, 1991). It is the responsibility of the college to provide the accommodation, and the responsibility of the student to make a timely and reasonable request (Brinckerhoff, Shaw, & McGuire, 2001). The George Washington University HEATH Resource Center (2003) provided an excellent breakdown of the specific roles of individuals involved in the accommodation process. They are listed as follows:

STUDENT ROLE

▶ Notify the faculty or Disability Services Office of your need for academic adjustments.

- Provide medical, psychological, and/or educational documentation to the DSS office.
- Participate in the process of determining and implementing appropriate academic adjustments.
- Inform the DSS office when academic adjustments are not working or need to be modified.

FACULTY ROLE

- Refer student to DSS Office.
- Participate in the process of determining and implementing appropriate academic adjustments.
- Identify course components for academic adjustments to be determined.
- Request assistance from the DSS office with respect to implementation of academic adjustments.

STUDENT DISABILITY SERVICES OFFICE ROLE

- Maintain medical, education, and/or psychological documentation in a confidential manner.
- Determine if condition(s) is a disability in accordance with state and federal laws.
- Identify and assist with implementation of appropriate academic adjustments.
- Request updated documentation as needed to determine if academic adjustments need to be modified.
- Provide information and referral to campus and community resources to resolve disability related issues. (HEATH Resource Center, 2003, p. 56)

SELECTING APPROPRIATE ACCOMMODATIONS

Determining which accommodations would benefit you is not a decision that should be taken without critically analyzing your needs. The Disability Services Office will assist you in determining which accommodations will support you in the college setting. Students with disabilities may have challenges with auditory, visual, or tactile information. It may take longer for some students who have learning difficulties to process written information or to complete lengthy reading assignments while others may have difficulties focusing on tasks, organizing their materials, or managing their time. For example, if you are a student who has a difficult time attending in class, but can complete the work successfully if you had all of the information shared in class, one or more of the following accommodations may benefit you:

- use of a tape recorder or assistive listening device;
- use of a note-taker (e.g., another student in the class);
- copy of the instructor's notes;
- permission to record lectures; and
- alternate testing environment (separate room or with a small group of students).

If you struggle to complete lengthy written assignments or essay exams because of difficulties with the writing process, or you become easily distracted, one or more of the following accommodations may benefit you:

- graphic organizer software;
- access to assistive technology devices (e.g., completing all work on a computer);
- altered test formats (e.g., oral response, dictating);
- a quiet work location; and
- extra time on assignments and tests.

If reading and processing written language is a difficult task for you, one or more of the following accommodations needs to be considered:

- a quiet work location;
- reduced length of reading assignment;

- ► extra time on assignments and tests; and
- ► books on tape.

Although the above lists do not include all of the accommodations that a student may request, understanding the characteristics of your own disability and the areas of difficulty that may be challenging for you as a college student will help in deciding on the accommodations that will provide the most benefits as you pursue a college degree.

In addition, there are other accommodations that can be included in your program that may not occur in specific classes but will have a major impact on the success of your educational experience. For example, some colleges give specific timelines as to the length of time students are permitted to complete their degree (e.g., 4 years). This may not be a reasonable timeline for students who need to have a reduction in the course load each semester as an accommodation. Therefore, this would need to be negotiated at the beginning of your program. Also, because of a specific disability, you may need to request a substitution for a specific course that is considered a nonstandard substitution. Again, it would be up to the college to decide if this substitution would jeopardize the integrity of the program of study or be a reasonable accommodation in order to provide you with an equal opportunity to achieve equal results.

If a student makes a request for an accommodation that the college does not feel constitutes a "reasonable accommodation," the college can propose an alternative accommodation. However, under Section 504, students with learning disabilities are entitled to "equivalent access" to the educational environment, but the student needs to be willing to work with the college in coming to a reasonable consensus. Furthermore, if the proposed accommodation does not pose an undue financial or administrative burden on the institution or result in fundamental alterations in program requirements, then the institution must ultimately bear the costs of the accommodation (Brinckerhoff et al., 2001).

Additional information on accommodations for college students can be found at http://www.wrightslaw.com/info/sec504.college.accoms.brown.htm. This Web site includes legal information, as well as links to additional resources regarding accommodations and rights and responsibilities of the student and the college or university.

LEARNING TO ASK THE RIGHT QUESTIONS

1. Do you know which classroom and testing accommodations you require?
2. Do the accommodations you are requesting directly impact your ability to learn?
3. Do you understand the process for requesting accommodations?
4. Have you arranged a meeting with your instructor to discuss your academic accommodations?

DISCUSSING ACCOMMODATIONS WITH COLLEGE PROFESSORS

Once you have met with the Disability Service Coordinator, you should determine how and when you will share your accommodations with your instructors. It is highly recommended that students with disabilities, including learning disabilities, schedule an appointment early on with their instructors. If a teaching assistant (TA) is used for the course, you should request that the TA be present at the meeting. During this meeting, you should share the determined accommodations with your instructor and offer the opportunity for the instructor to provide further input as to his or her expectations in the class. It is imperative that you do not begin the meeting by demanding accommodations. A clear plan for the meeting should be established where you introduce yourself, explain that you have a documented disability, and talk about how this disability might affect your performance in the class. Although instructors should be familiar with specific disabilities, this is not always the case. Identifying some of the common characteristics of the disability and how they impact your ability to be successful in the classroom will provide the perfect opportunity to discuss the accommodations that were established with the Disability Service Coordinator and how such accommodations will allow you to overcome possible obstacles within the classroom. Most importantly, students should take ownership of their responsibilities within the class. These responsibilities should be expressed to the instructor, as well, and should include taking necessary actions to schedule appointments with the instructor when having difficulty with content or assessments for the course.

You should establish collegial relationships with your instructors early on so that you can feel more comfortable discussing any problems that may arise. In the college setting, you will take many courses and this process should be repeated with each instructor. If you do not share your accommodations with the instructor early on, he or she will not be prepared to provide the necessary accommodations. However, when you're upfront and honest about your accommodation needs, most instructors are willing to go above and beyond providing the basic accommodations. For example, instructors who have students in the class who need copies of notes often will post notes to Blackboard™ or WebCT™ prior to lectures. Some instructors may even offer suggestions to the student such as participating in study groups or tutorials.

EXPLAINING ACCOMMODATIONS
TO FRIENDS AND CLASSMATES

As in the high school setting, peers or other classmates may notice that a student is getting what is perceived as special privileges. This perception may lead to confrontations by a classmate. In this situation, it is best to be upfront and honest. For example, if you are given the accommodation of sitting close to the front of the classroom and seem to have better access to the professor, you may have to explain that if you do not sit there, you will be easily distracted or unable to focus on the material presented. Typically this is enough. More often, this situation does not arise in the instructional setting but rather in study groups or when meeting with assigned partners. In this situation, it is recommended that you carefully evaluate the situation and determine if you should disclose your disability to your study peers.

If you do choose to share your specific disability, you should be prepared to state not only how this might challenge you in the group situation, but also what benefits you can contribute to the group. For example, if a student with a specific learning disability has difficulty with written expression, he or she should explain to the group that this may not be the best task for him. However, the same student may have developed excellent skills using specific software programs such as Microsoft PowerPoint and can contribute by assisting with the design or presentation of the materials. Sharing your strengths with classmates will help your peers to more openly accept you for what you have to offer, not what challenges may be imposed on the group.

GRIEVANCE PROCEDURES

As stated earlier, most instructors know that students with disabilities are protected under the law, and that they are expected to provide the instructional accommodations for their students (Eckes & Ochoa, 2005). However, in a situation where you do not feel that the accommodations are being implemented, you will need to contact the Disability Service Coordinator. Hopefully, the coordinator will be able to resolve the issue with the instructor. As a general rule, disability grievance should be handled internally in efforts to resolve the issue. However, if internal grievance procedures do not resolve your complaint, you should contact the U.S. Department of Education Office for Civil Rights and complete the process for filing a complaint (see http://www.ed.gov/about/offices/list/ocr/complaintprocess.html for more information). In many cases, OCR complaints must be filed within 180 days of the alleged discrimination. If you determine that filing a claim is necessary, it is important to be prepared with appropriate documentation that proves the discrimination occurred.

LEARNING TO ASK THE RIGHT QUESTIONS

1. Who is the person to contact at the university you are attending if you feel you are being discriminated against because of your disability?
2. Have you read through the grievance process located at the Office for Civil Rights Web site?
3. Have you met with the instructor and informed him or her that you feel your accommodations are not being met?

CONCLUSION

Because the goal of attending a postsecondary institution is to receive a college degree, this chapter contains some of the most important information for you as a prospective college student. As a student with a disability, you need to have an understanding of your own strengths and limitations and be proactive in obtaining the necessary services that will assist you in meeting your academic needs. This means that you will have to make the decision on whether or not to disclose your disability; however, if you needed academic supports while you were in high school, there is a good chance that you will need them in college as well. Because of the increased responsibilities that will be placed on you, having people who can support you within this new academic environment can be the defining reason for success.

There is much more to college than just signing up for courses. Knowing and understanding yourself as a learner will help you develop an educational plan along with the support of your academic advisor and the Student Disability Services Office. They will be able to assist you in identifying the most appropriate accommodations, knowing how to discuss those accommodations with your professors, and knowing what process to follow if those accommodations are not being implemented in all of your classes. Seeing yourself as a capable and effective learner and being willing to self-advocate for your academic needs are essential to your achievement.

STUDENT INTERVIEWS

When were you assigned an academic advisor and when was your first meeting?

James: I was assigned an advisor at the beginning of my freshman year and I met with her well before classes began. I really wanted to be prepared and take the correct courses for my degree plan, so it was good to start early. An advisor is a very important mentor to any student, but especially those with disabilities. During the first meeting, we used a generic degree plan to develop a long-term outline of the courses I would take over the next 4 years. My advisor makes sure I follow my degree plan and informs me of the basic services that are available; however she is not very familiar with the Disability Services Office, so she recommended I visit them to explain and request services based on my disability.

What information did your advisor share during that first meeting?

James: She explained the importance of following your degree plan. She cautioned against dropping any courses, because it wastes time and money. Because of this, it is very important to carefully select your degree plan and courses. Also, she explained a lot of additional information regarding the teaching program at SHSU including any specific requirements and coursework that applied to my own program of study.

Angela: I don't remember exactly what we discussed at our first meeting, but I know we determined what classes I would need to take and discussed the course load decision.

How did you decide on the appropriate course load for you?

James: At first, I chose the minimum amount for full time, because I wanted to ease myself into the demands of college coursework. As I look back, it was a good choice because it enabled me to focus on adjusting to college life without being overwhelmed. My advice would be to take the least amount of hours you possibly can, while still progressing through your degree plan. One strategy I used was that I would take less hours in the fall and spring and make up the difference in the summer. The important point to remember is that you should make the decision based on what you are comfortable with.

What process do you use in advocating for yourself in your courses?

James: I always try to communicate with my professors in a professional and honest manner regarding my needs and my disability. The process at my university is quite simple and it takes very little time to request the accommodations. First, I visit the Disability Services Office and provide them with information regarding my diagnosis, as well as my impression of what I need to succeed at SHSU. Then the office prepares accommodations forms for each of my professors, which I have to deliver, explain, and return signed. If a professor has reasonable questions to ask me about my accommodations, I will do whatever I can to explain things and clarify my needs. The three key points to remember are: Be honest, be flexible, and be reasonable.

Has there been anything particularly helpful for you that professors have done that is currently not part of your required accommodations?

James: The most helpful thing any professor has done in regard to my accommodations is his or her willingness to openly discuss my disability and listen to my concerns. Sometimes they have even thought of better and more efficient ways to provide an accommodation. The professors are required to provide certain accommodations, but the list is not exhaustive and can be expanded upon or modified with your consent. For example, an accommodation I utilize frequently is the assistance of a volunteer student note-taker. After reading my form, my math professor offered to simply make copies of her lecture notes for me, in exchange for my attempt to do my best to take notes and use her notes only as a study tool. This arrangement worked very well for me and I expressed my appreciation to that professor at the end of the course.

Was there a particularly type of teaching style that worked best for you?

Angela: Visual styles, as well as group work, seem to work best for me, because I need to be able to see things in order to understand them. For instance, lectures are very hard for me because I cannot process what the professor is saying in order to take notes. Also, when I am able to picture something I can understand it.

STUDY SKILLS CHECKLIST

	Yes	No	Some
Do I know how to research in a library?			
Do I know how to research online?			
Do I know how to research using an online library?			
Do I know how and when to seek tutorial assistance?			
Can I take notes from a lecture by hand?			
Can I take notes from a computer?			
Can I take notes from a tape recording?			
Do I know how to takes notes from a book?			
Do I know how to takes notes from a video course?			
Do I know how to take notes from an online course?			
Do I know how to mark important information in my reading passages?			
Do I know how to study for different kinds of tests?			
Do I know how to take different kinds of tests?			
Do I need extra time for tests?			
Am I usually prepared for class?			
Am I usually on time for class?			
Do I skip classes often?			
Are my schoolwork and notes neat?			
Am I good at organizing my work (e.g., folders, computer files, etc.)?			
Do I organize my notes effectively (e.g., note-books for each class, dividers, highlighting, color-coding)?			
Are my assignments completed on time?			
Is my behavior in class appropriate and not distracting to others?			
Do I stay focused in class?			
Can I do my share of a group project?			

Note. Adapted from WNY College Consortium and Disability Advocates (n.d.).

WEB SITES RELATED TO CHAPTER 5

LDOnline

http://www.ldonline.org

This site provides information on college preparation for students with learning disabilities.

High School Students With LD or AD/HD: Considering College

http://www.greatschools.net/cgi-bin/showarticle/2975

This article provides guidelines for making an informed decision about attending college.

How to Study: A Study Skills Resource Site

http://www.how-to-study.com

This Web site addresses all aspects of developing study skills, with free access to a variety of study skill programs and guides in both English and Spanish.

College Students and Disability Law

http://www.ldonline.org/article/6082

This Web site addresses legal protection for students with disabilities attending college.

Post ITT

http://www.postitt.org/activities/index.shtml

This site provides guidance activities designed for high school students. Separate modules are available for parents.

WNY Collegiate Consortium and Disability Advocates

http://www.ccdanet.org

This site provides information on issues for students with disabilities transitioning into postsecondary education.

University of Nebraska-Lincoln Cognitive Strategy Instruction: Written Composition

http://www.unl.edu/csi/wcomp.html

This site provides sample graphic organizers for completing writing assignments.

University of Nebraska-Lincoln Cognitive Strategy Instruction: Note Taking

http://www.unl.edu/csi/notes.html

This site provides information on note-taking strategies.

[ADAPTING TO UNIVERSITY LIFE]

F**EW** people would argue that the college experience involves just attending classes. Just ask any college student. Students are only in class for a small amount of time each week, and part of the college experience is being able to explore interests beyond academics. Most postsecondary institutions provide students with a wealth of information from academics to student life on their Web site. This information may have played a role in helping students choose the college or university that seemed to be the best fit. Once classes start, you will want to explore opportunities in which you can pursue your own interests.

EXPLORING CAMPUS LIFE

Attending freshman orientation is a good first step to discover ways to get involved in campus life, but you have to make the first move in actually getting involved. Most campuses have a campus life or student affairs office that will provide detailed information on all of the activities and organizations offered at the university. These offices often host Web sites that include a listing of the contact information for organizations along with possible meeting dates and times. Many organizations also advertise new member meetings or information sessions on bulletin boards and sidewalk chalkings across campus. You can use lists of organizations and advertisements as sources to determine what opportunities are available to you. Then, it is up to you to take the next step.

Typically, universities offer a wide array of activities for students to investigate. Standard opportunities include involvement choices focusing on:

- ▶ service,
- ▶ specific interest areas,
- ▶ academics,
- ▶ cultural activities,
- ▶ social interaction (fraternities or sororities),
- ▶ religion,
- ▶ honors programming (honor societies), and
- ▶ student governance (student body officers, student courts).

Obviously, the names of specific organizations will vary from campus to campus. However, some organizations like Habitat for Humanity (service-based), Future Farmers of America (interest-based), Golden Key International Honor Society (honors-based), and Young Life (religious) are national organizations with college chapters. Some universities also house local organizations, particular to just that university or to a region or consortium of universities. No matter what you choose, every university has a myriad of opportunities available for student involvement.

With so many opportunities available, you will have to make some choices regarding how many activities and organizations you can join. You need to be cautious about becoming too involved before knowing how much free time you will have in your academic schedule. Each semester, you will want to reevaluate your level of involvement. Often, students with disabilities find that some semesters require them to limit the amount of time they are involved in extracurricular activities, while other semesters may allow more time for involvement. Keep in mind that some universities limit student involvement during the first semester; for example, some schools do not allow first-semester students to join time-intensive groups such as sororities and fraternities.

Active participation in campus life and all that it offers is an important part of the postsecondary experience and also may help you avoid the isolation that can occur, especially if it is your first time to live away from your home. Extracurricular activities also provide students with opportunities to connect with other students who have similar interests.

TIME MANAGEMENT

Managing one's time can be a difficult task for any college student. This holds especially true for students with identified disabilities. Finding a healthy balance between academics and activities is essential in a successful college experience. You need to schedule a specific time each day for studying. The designated time should be chosen based on when you are the most alert. This time may vary each day depending on your class schedule. You also should study your most difficult or least favorite subject first. Studying for the most difficult subject first will allow you greater opportunity to focus. Those students who have difficulty maintaining focus may need to take frequent breaks during studying.

Using a planner will help you keep up with your assignments. Many students begin each semester by setting up a detailed schedule that is too difficult to follow and give up the scheduling idea completely. You can establish a daily, weekly, and semester-long schedule using an academic planner.

Academic planners allow students to see the entire semester at a glance and know that some activities are fixed and will not be changed. At the same time, seeing the entire semester at a glance can sometimes be overwhelming in regard to how much has to be accomplished before the semester ends, so approaching the semester one week at a time gives you a little more control. However, in order to effectively manage your time, you must organize your time on a daily basis that fits into your weeklong plan. The following example is a method of organizing time that has been helpful to many students with and without disabilities.

1. *Long-Term Schedule*: At the beginning of the semester, write in your fixed schedule. This includes classes, job hours, organization meetings, and other regular commitments.

2. *Weekly Schedule*: On Sunday evening each week, write in all of the assignments that you need to complete or work on and any nonacademic activities you plan to attend. These will change each week, so this will need to be completed each Sunday evening. For example:

> Club meeting Monday night
> Read Chapter 9 in history by Wednesday
> Develop outline for math project by Thursday
> English quiz on Friday

3. *Daily Schedule*: Before going to bed each evening, make out a specific daily schedule for the following day. Enter what has to be completed, and don't forget to add in study time. A daily schedule might include:

9:00–9:45 a.m.	Review for English quiz
2:00–3:30 p.m.	Read Chapter 9 in history
3:45–5:00 p.m.	Library—work on math project
7:30–9:30 p.m.	Organizational meeting
11:00–11:15 p.m.	Review rest of week and fill in tomorrow's schedule

Some additional examples of a weekly and monthly calendar/planner can be found in the Resources Section at the end of the chapter.

DEVELOPING GOOD STUDY HABITS

Another part of time management is deciding where to study. You must first determine what kind of setting is most conducive to your personal study habits. For example, a student with ADHD may need a quiet environment with no distractions. If this is the case, then the dormitory is probably not an option. Another consideration is whether or not you have a computer in your dorm room. If a computer is not available, you may need to study in a computer lab setting. The environment a student chooses to study in may vary across courses. This is common; however, you will need to be able to self-monitor the effectiveness of each setting you choose.

Many students with disabilities such as ADHD or learning disabilities have indicated that it is helpful to participate in study groups, while some students with disabilities such as Asperger's syndrome may have difficulty working in this situation. Working in small groups involves a vast array of social skills. Study groups can be helpful in allowing students to discuss and clarify concepts that have been covered in class. Typically, study groups are developed through an informal process of just asking other students in the class if they are interested in getting together outside of class to cover the material. For some students, the opportunity to talk about the content can be an effective strategy for learning and reinforcing new material, although some students with disabilities find it difficult to make connections with peers in the classroom setting. Students should check with the professor to determine if he or she is aware of a study group taking place.

Often, the office of student services or the counseling center will offer specific instruction in critical elements such as working as a team member, active and critical listening skills, accepting constructive feedback, managing time, understanding expectations of the team, and forming friendships. In addition, students without disabilities in the group may not clearly understand your limitations or specific disabilities. Most college students with disabilities that we interviewed felt strongly that in order to successfully participate in small groups they needed to disclose and explain their disability to their peers. During the explanation, students were able to identify not only their limitations, but also were given the opportunity to discuss how their particular strengths would benefit the group.

In addition to participation in study groups, keeping up with the assigned readings and assignments is essential to managing one's time. Even the most effective study plan is not going to work if you do not follow it through. It is difficult for most students to play catch-up if they start falling behind. This is especially true for students with disabilities. If you develop a plan that provides a balance between academics and activities, you are less likely to feel overwhelmed and more likely to have a successful semester. Many postsecondary institutions provide services that assist students in time management, as mentioned in the previous chapter.

LEARNING TO ASK THE RIGHT QUESTIONS

1. Do you know what activities or organizations you would like to be involved in? How much time would your participation take?
2. Are you good at managing your time?
3. Do you know how to use a planner for daily, weekly, and long-term assignments?
4. Do you know how to schedule time for academic tasks while leaving time for extracurricular activities?
5. What type of setting is most conducive to your study habits?
6. What social skills are necessary to participate in a study group?

SOCIAL ISSUES

Although the focus of college is academics, the reality is that college is about personal growth and discovery. Making new friends and engaging in social activities is an important part of campus life and the college experience. Despite one's social skills abilities or disabilities, there are many new social challenges facing college students. With the frequent changing of class schedules, living situations, and long semester breaks, there is minimal consistency in remaining with the same group of people for any length of time. Yet, a key factor in making friends is spending time together. Planning activities with friends also will be a part of managing one's time. Again, you have to find the balance between academics and your social life. Students with social deficits may find this aspect of the college experience extremely difficult.

Understanding the effects of your disability and how it plays into your social interactions will better prepare you to adjust to the new social environment. "Reading and understanding cultural rules is necessary to life beyond college while understanding more subtle social cues and being able to manage one's impulses to act appropriately can be the fine line between fitting in or being isolated" (Quinn, Ratey, & Maitland, 2000, p. 114). Because of the novelty of being on a college campus and all of the freedom that offers, students need to make a conscious effort in choosing friends. By attending campus activities, you can identify with other students who have similar interests. This also will allow you to fill unstructured time with university-approved activities. Students with disabilities who suffer from depression may struggle with "down time." Students who have too much free time may find themselves becoming involved with students who participate in questionable activities.

One of the most important social situations that you will be faced with is the possibility of living with a roommate. This can be challenging for any student, but it can be especially daunting for a student who has a disability that is characterized by social deficits. It will be up to you to decide whether or not you want to disclose the disability to your roommate, but it may make for an easier adjustment if your roommate has a basic understanding of your disability and how it may affect your social skills.

You also will be interacting daily with people who are placed in various roles of authority. This will include professors, dorm staff, and other campus personnel across the college community. Because of the new social environment, social skills training needs to be a part of the transition plan while you are still in high school. This will provide an opportunity for you to role-play some of the social situations that will occur once you are living on a college campus (see Chapter 2). If you find yourself struggling with social issues or any other personal issues, most colleges provide counseling services that can offer assistance.

COUNSELING SERVICES

The majority of college campuses offer counseling services that are staffed by professionals and provide most services free of charge. Prior to entering college, you should know what assistance is available to you, and that you are not alone in learning to adapt to your new environment. Some stress will be expected as you adjust to your new life, but you may need additional support from the counseling office to understand how to best cope with these changes. A complete change in routine, lifestyle, and eating and sleeping habits, and isolation from family and old friends can be overwhelming for all students, but it can be especially difficult for students with disabilities who may have had a number of supports in place before heading off to college. You can contact the university counseling office directly to discuss what type of assistance it provides. Some healthy stress management techniques for all college students include:

- getting plenty of sleep,
- sticking to your weekly planner,
- exercising on a regular basis,
- listening to your body,
- eating a healthy diet, and
- having healthy relationships.

Engaging in good health practices and setting healthy boundaries are effective means of stress prevention. Dealing with stress in a constructive way will enable you to have a more balanced, healthy, and productive college experience.

LEARNING TO ASK THE RIGHT QUESTIONS

1. How do you choose your friends?
2. Do you know how to interact with people in authority?
3. Does the Student Disability Services Office offer support services directly related to social acceptance?
4. Are specific activities offered through the Student Disability Services Office that involve the opportunity to interact with other individuals with disabilities similar to your own?
5. Do you know how to identify the causes of your stress?
6. Do you know what stress management techniques work best for you?

CONCLUSION

As any college student will attest, academics are only part of the college experience. You will be making new friends and hopefully pursing other areas of interest outside of academia. College can be a lonely time for first-semester freshmen as they often are living away from home for the first time. Fortunately, you can go to the campus life or student affairs office to explore the many opportunities that are available, but you have to find a balance between school work and your social life.

For college students in general, time management can be challenging. Developing a time management system, which should involve some type of planner or calendar, will be essential in helping you manage your time. However, this plan will not work unless you follow through. It can become very easy to spend your time with new friends and push academics aside. At the same time, you can become overwhelmed with trying to manage your new life and you may need some additional assistance. Most colleges provide counseling services that can assist students in adapting to their new environment. College is about personal growth and discovery and asking for additional support can be a healthy response to this new college experience.

STUDENT INTERVIEWS

How did you find out about campus life activities and organizations?

James: I found information about campus activities through two different sources. The first was through my professors in the College of Education. They provided information about different education-related organizations by having representatives visit our classes and by giving us literature on them. The other way I learned about activities and organizations was through the Student Activities Department, which serves as a resource on all campus activities and student organizations. They provide a campus calendar at the beginning of every semester, and they also maintain an active listing of all organizations and their contact information. Because my university has so many organizations, it is very useful to have a way to filter through all of the information. In addition, my university hosts several events each semester that feature different campus organization booths that disseminate information.

How did you choose what organizations to join?

James: I primarily chose organizations that were related to my major, but I also became involved in honor societies and civic organizations. The organizations related to my degree were great because they taught me very useful information for my future classroom and connected me to my colleagues in other education classes. Based on my personal commitment to academic excellence, I chose to be involved with honor societies to find ways to get involved with other leaders and to demonstrate my commitment. The biggest piece of advice I could give would be to pick organizations that you know you will enjoy and to remember that if you begin to see an organization as an obligation instead of a personal commitment, it is time to move on. An organization is meant to enhance your college experience, not make it more difficult or stressful.

Were you involved in campus life activities and organizations?

Angela: I attended Texas State Teacher Association (TSTA) and Sam Houston Council for Exceptional Children (SCEC) meetings. I attended a lot of sports events and made a lot of friends. I wanted to be involved in activities where there would be people who had the same interests as I do, and I also wanted to learn more about my degree and topics related to my interests.

What has been the most helpful in finding a balance between academics and activities?

James: At first, they were very difficult to balance, but I was determined to make it work. The best method I found to find a balance was using a schedule planner. I would input all of the days and times of my organization meetings and events and look for conflicts between my classes. Sometimes, I had to accept that I couldn't go to a certain event or meeting because class should and must come first, but I would try to make it up in some way.

For instance, if I missed one meeting, I would make certain that I was at the next one. One important point I would stress is that you should remember the quality of your involvement is much more important than the quantity. It is better to be an active and dedicated member of one or two organizations than an inactive member of several.

How did you go about keeping a schedule of your daily, weekly, and semester-long activities?

James: I rely heavily on a day planner to enable me to keep my schedule on track and current. If I write something in my planner, I am guaranteed to be there; if I don't remember to do this, I will simply forget, even if it's only a day later. I learned this skill in high school, and I have found it to be a lifesaver. I have accepted that I am very forgetful; however, I have learned to use my planner as an effective means of compensation for this. For other more tech-savvy people though, I would recommend the use of a PDA, electronic datebook, or an e-mail program, such as Microsoft Outlook. The main point is to use the method that works best for you. If you are unsure of what method to use, ask for help from a teacher or a counselor.

Angela: I religiously use a day planner and I always have multiple to-do and reminder lists going at all times. I tried to stay on top of my academics so that when the activities I wanted to participate in came up, I was able to take advantage of the opportunities and have fun instead of having to turn things down.

How did you go about developing friendships?

James: The most beneficial avenue for being successful in developing friendships was through my participation in organizations. The organizations provided a relaxed atmosphere for meeting people and socializing. I found this forum to be extremely helpful in developing friendly relationships during my freshman year. Once I became an officer in several of these organizations, they provided me with even more opportunities to make friends. I also met other people through networking with existing friends. Everyone is connected through different people and many of the friends I made were met through the friends of other friends. The best way to develop solid and lasting friendships is simply to be cordial and be willing to take risks, even if it's outside of your comfort zone. Go to a party, attend a football game, or go to a social dinner—all of these activities can lead to making more friends and opening up brand-new opportunities for friendship.

Angela: I already had a couple friends who attended SHSU before I got there, so I met their friends and also made friends of my own. I also met a lot of people who were taking the same classes.

SAMPLE MONTHLY CALENDAR/PLANNER
SEPTEMBER

Sunday	Monday	Tuesday	Wednesday	Thursday	Friday	Saturday
				1 Math Project Due 2–4 Library	2	3
4	5 6–8 Study Group	6	7	8 2–4 Library	9 Home for the Weekend	10 Home for the Weekend
11	12 6–8 Study Group	13	14 Science Exam	15 2–4 Library	16	17
18	19 6–8 Study Group	20	21	22 2–4 Library	23	24 Community Project
25	26 6–8 Study Group	27	28	29 2–4 Library	30	31

SAMPLE WEEKLY PLANNER

					Week of <u>Sept. 1–7</u>	
Date:	**English**	**Math**	**Science**	**Computer**	**Study Time**	**Other Activities**
Monday	8–9 a.m.		12–3 p.m.		7–9 p.m.	
Tuesday		11–1 p.m.		3–5 p.m.	8–10 p.m.	
Wednesday	8–9 a.m.		12–3 p.m.		7–9 p.m.	
Thursday		11–1 p.m.			8–10 p.m.	6–7 p.m. Drama Team Mtg.
Friday	Library (a.m.)			Free Time		Home for Weekend

Student should fill in academic assignments and extracurricular activities on their weekly calendar.

WEB SITES RELATED TO CHAPTER 6

COLLEGE GRAZING
http://www.collegegrazing.com
This site is designed to assist students in finding a college that fits their needs and provides many interactive planning tools.

COLLEGE SURVIVAL SKILLS
http://www.washington.edu/doit/Brochures/Academics/survival/html
This site provides tips for students with disabilities to increase college success.

TEACHING TIME MANAGEMENT TO STUDENTS WITH LEARNING DISABILITIES
http://www.ldonline.org/article/23676
This article contains information and an activity that addresses time-management issues for students with LD.

FINAL THOUGHTS

THE information in this book is the result of progress that those in the field of education are slowly making in expanding the opportunities for students with LD and other disabilities to pursue a postsecondary education. College is a possibility! If you are a student with a disability, you can no longer assume that college is not an option.

Early planning and preparation is a key factor in a successful transition from high school to college. You can use this book as a guide to obtain the needed information and assist you in meeting the timelines along the way. If you need assistance with the process, talk with your parents, teachers, or a school counselor who can provide the additional support you may need to remain focused and on track.

As is evidenced throughout the book, it takes time and a commitment to fulfill all of the necessary requirements to get a letter of acceptance, but the work does not stop there. Granted, it is your decision to decide whether or not you will disclose your disability to the college, but considering all of the changes that college brings, the continued support provided by the Student Disability Services Office can have a positive impact on your college experience. Just as you had support during your public school years, colleges also are prepared to offer the necessary accommodations. Use them to your advantage. Those accommodations are only in place to level the playing field.

Remember, you are your own biggest advocate. Set goals and pursue them. Ask questions. Seek answers. Follow through. Work hard and enjoy your life as a college student!

Glossary
of Terms

ACADEMIC ACHIEVEMENT: refers to how a student is performing academically.

ACADEMIC ADVISOR: a person on staff at the college or university that assists students in the development of their educational plan.

ACCOMMODATION: a modification to the delivery of instruction or method of student performance that does not significantly change the content or curriculum.

ACT: a college entrance exam that assesses high school students' general educational development and their ability to complete college-level work.

ADVOCACY: speaking up for a cause, person, or idea.

AMERICANS WITH DISABILITIES ACT OF 1990 (ADA): a civil rights law that provides equal access and opportunity and prevents discriminations for students with disabilities.

ASPERGER'S SYNDROME: a developmental disorder that affects a person's ability to socialize and communicate effectively with others.

ASSISTIVE TECHNOLOGY: equipment, hardware, inventions, tools, or other assistance for people with disabilities; aids to help people do the tasks of daily life.

ATTENTION DEFICIT HYPERACTIVITY DISORDER (ADHD): a condition characterized by problems of inattention, hyperactivity, and/or impulsivity.

BLACKBOARD™ OR WEBCT™: interactive online learning systems designed to enhance teaching and learning through the use of software applications.

CAREER CENTER: a resource area in a high school that will assist students in learning about careers and postsecondary institutions; many universities have career centers for postcollege career advice and guidance.

COLLEGE BOARD: a not-for-profit examination board that manages the administration of nationwide aptitude and achievement tests used by most U.S. colleges and universities as part of their admissions process.

COMPENSATION STRATEGIES: methods and techniques to provide students support in areas of deficits.

COURSE OF STUDY: an academic framework that includes the courses needed to complete a certification or degree program.

DAILY LIVING SKILLS: the basic activities of daily living such as self-care, work, homemaking, and leisure.

DISABILITY SERVICE COORDINATOR: a staff member on the college or university campus who assists the student in accessing the needed services for academic success.

EDUCATIONAL DIAGNOSTICIANS: professionals who assess and diagnose the learning problems of students.

EQUAL EMPLOYMENT OPPORTUNITY COMMISSION (EEOC): a federal agency in charge of administration and judicial enforcement of the federal civil rights laws.

EXTRACURRICULAR ACTIVITIES: activities performed by students that are not part of the normal school curriculum and can include a range of clubs, organizations, and team sports.

FAMILY EDUCATIONAL RIGHTS AND PRIVACY ACT OF 1974 (FERPA): a U.S. federal law that protects the confidentiality of student education records.

FOUR-YEAR INSTITUTION: referred to as a college, university, or postsecondary institution that provides students with a 4-year program of collegiate academic study.

FUNCTIONAL ACHIEVEMENT: refers to how a student is performing skills in daily living, personal and social interactions, and employability.

FUNCTIONAL VOCATIONAL EVALUATION: an assessment process that is an organized approach to identifying the interests, needs, preferences, and abilities that an individual student has in the domain of occupational/employability skills.

GRADE POINT AVERAGE (GPA): the student's cumulative grades.

INDEPENDENT LIVING: the ability to live on one's own.

INDIVIDUAL WITH DISABILITIES EDUCATION IMPROVEMENT ACT (IDEA): a law ensuring services to children with disabilities throughout the nation. IDEA governs how states and public agencies provide early intervention, special education, and related services to more than 6.5 million eligible infants, toddlers, children, and youth with disabilities.

INDIVIDUALIZED EDUCATION PROGRAM (IEP): a written document that ensures that a child with a disability receives a free, appropriate education in the least restrictive environment; designed to meet the individual needs of a student with a disability.

INSTRUCTIONAL STRATEGIES: methods, materials, and techniques that can be used to assist students in strengthening their own areas of academic need, thereby enhancing the learning process.

INTEGRATED EMPLOYMENT: a job where a person with disabilities has real work opportunities in a setting where most employees are nondisabled.

LEARNED HELPLESSNESS: a person learns to act or behave helpless in a particular situation.

LEARNING DISABILITIES (LD): a term that describes specific kinds of learning problems that affect a broad range of academic skills including reading, writing, listening, speaking, mathematics, and reasoning abilities.

LEARNING STYLES: conditions under which a student is most likely to learn. This may be through a combination of any of the senses.

LETTER OF RECOMMENDATION: a letter written by a teacher, counselor, or someone well-respected in the community who can talk about the student's personal qualities, accomplishments, and experiences that may have not been discussed in the student's college or job application.

OFFICE FOR CIVIL RIGHTS: a federal agency that prohibits discrimination in educational programs and activities receiving federal financial assistance.

POSTSECONDARY EDUCATION: educational institutions beyond high school that have an academic, vocational, or professional focus.

PRIVATE COLLEGE OR UNIVERSITY: postsecondary school that is supported and run by a private agency; private schools typically charge higher tuition and have smaller enrollments than public schools.

PROGRESS MONITORING: collecting and using data to frequently check students' progress toward success.

PUBLIC COLLEGE OR UNIVERSITY: postsecondary school that is supported by public funds; provides reduced tuition for students who are citizens of the state that supports it.

RELATED SERVICES: services a student with disabilities needs in order to benefit from special education and may include, but are not limited to, speech therapy, physical therapy, and occupational therapy.

RESEARCH-BASED INTERVENTIONS: instructional strategies that have been proven through research to enhance student learning.

RESIDENT ASSISTANT (RA): a trained leader within a college or university responsible for supervising students in a residence hall (dorm).

RESPONSE TO INTERVENTION (RTI): an alternative method of identifying learning disabilities using early intervention, frequent progress monitoring, and the use of intensive research-based instructional strategies.

SAT REASONING TEST: formerly known as the Scholastic Aptitude Test; a standardized test for admissions into U.S. colleges and universities.

SCHOOL PSYCHOLOGIST: a psychologist who specializes in the assessment and problems of school-age children.

SECTION 504: a civil rights law that is part of the Rehabilitation Act of 1973; provides equal access and opportunity and prevents discrimination for persons with disabilities.

SELF-ADVOCACY: the ability to communicate one's talents, skills, and needed accommodations to others.

SELF-DETERMINATION: enables individuals to take responsibilities for their lives at school and within the community.

SELF-MONITORING: involves the student monitoring his or her own progress in the effort to develop a skill or complete a project.

SOCIAL SKILLS: a set of social rules and regulations that people need to effectively communicate and interact with others.

STUDENT DISABILITY SERVICES OFFICE (SDSO): an office on the college or university campus that provides services and supports for students with disabilities; also referred to as Disability Services Office or Disability Support Services on some campuses.

TRANSITION PLANNING: the process of planning for a student's future as he or she moves from high school into adult life.

TRANSITION SERVICES: services that include strategies and activities that will assist the student in preparing for postsecondary activities once he or she leaves high school.

TWO-YEAR INSTITUTION: often referred to as a community college or junior college; provides students with a 2-year program of collegiate academic study.

U.S. DEPARTMENT OF JUSTICE: a department in the U.S. government designed to enforce the law and defend the interests of all Americans according to the law and to ensure fair and impartial administration of justice.

VOCATIONAL REHABILITATION AGENCY: provides a variety of services that focus on career development, employment preparation, achieving independence, and integration in the workplace and community for people with disabilities.

VOCATIONAL TRAINING: training at the high school or postsecondary level to provide students with work experience for future employment.

ADDITIONAL WEB SITE RESOURCES

2007 CREATING OPTIONS: FINANCIAL AID INFORMATION

http://www.heath.gwu.edu/files/active/0/creating_options_2007.pdf

The HEATH Resource Center's revised resource guide contains completely updated information to help individuals with disabilities to seek and obtain financial assistance for postsecondary education. The guide describes federal financial aid programs, state vocational rehabilitation services, and regional and local sources.

COLLEGES, COLLEGE SCHOLARSHIPS, AND ONLINE DEGREES

http://www.college-scholarships.com

This site provides easy access to information about colleges and universities located across the U.S., free scholarship and financial aid searches, SAT and ACT test prep tips, and online degrees and distance learning. It contains a directory of pertinent college and university information such as links to homepages, admission office e-mail address and phone numbers, as well as links to online applications.

COLLEGE FUNDING STRATEGIES
FOR STUDENTS WITH DISABILITIES

http://www.washington.edu/doit/Brochures/Academics/
financial-aid.html

The DO-IT Web site is a resource designed to show individuals and their families how to meet college costs through a combination of financial aid and other outside funding resources. It contains information describing federal student aid programs, SSI and PASS Programs, State Vocational Rehabilitation Services, and scholarships. It also contains links to financial aid and general and disability-related scholarships lists. The site itself is designed to be universally accessible. It has minimized the use of graphics and photos and provides descriptions of them when they are included. Video clips are captioned, providing access to users who can't hear the audio, and audio-described for those who cannot see the visual display.

EXPLORE FINANCIAL AID OPTIONS

http://mappingyourfuture.org/paying/financialaid.htm

Mapping Your Future is designed to enable individuals to achieve lifelong success by empowering schools, students, and families with free, Web-based college, financial aid, career, and financial literacy information and services. It provides resources for students and families, including career selection, early awareness, college planning, and money management tools and contains neutral content, encouraging students to look at all sources of free funding before considering a student loan. The Online Student Loan Counseling meets regulatory requirements and does not limit student choice of lenders and/or guarantors.

FAMILY AND COLLEGE FINANCES

http://moneycentral.msn.com/family/home.asp

The Family and College Finances section of the MSN Money Web site provides information regarding college savings plans (such as the 529 college savings plan) and how to find help with your college finance needs. It contains a tuition savings calculator (designed to guide you in saving for tuition) and a handy college and scholarship search section.

FinAid: The SmartStudent Guide to Financial Aid

http://www.finaid.com

FinAid: The SmartStudent Guide to Financial Aid contains "how to" guidance on securing financial aid. The site allows the user to create a profile and search for scholarships based upon the provided information. It provides information about secondary financial aid such as free scholarship lotteries, student profile-based aid, and aid for specific activities. As well as educating the users about the difference between various loans like PLUS, Perkins, and Stafford, FinAid helps to demystify the mountains of paperwork. It even gives tips to assist in maximizing financial aid eligibility. The site discusses different college savings plans and the best way to save.

Peterson's College Search

http://www.petersons.com/ugchannel/code/searches/srchCrit1. asp

The Peterson's College Search Web site contains information to assist in finding the colleges and universities of your dreams. It assists in planning by searching for the best colleges that fit who the student is and what he or she is looking for. It boasts an extensive database, making up a complete college guide of schools throughout the world. Users can search for a college based upon basic traits (size, location, cost, religious affiliation), student body (male-female ratio, diversity), academics (degrees, majors, special programs), and campus life (sports, clubs, fraternities, sororities).

RESOURCES FOR STUDENTS WITH DISABILITIES IN NEED OF FINANCIAL ASSISTANCE

http://www.icdri.org/Financial%20Aid/finaid.htm

This Web site contains resources to assist parents of students with disabilities and the students themselves who are looking for college financial aid and or student financial aid. It posts links to other sites such as the Vocational Rehabilitation Directors site. This U.S. Department of Labor program helps people who have physical, mental, or emotional disabilities get and keep a job. This can and does include payment for appropriate education and other services to qualify for and secure successful employment. The site also contains numerous links to obtain information about scholarships and financial aid.

ASSOCIATION ON HIGHER EDUCATION AND DISABILITY (AHEAD)

http://www.ahead.org

AHEAD is a professional membership organization for individuals involved in the development of policy and in the provision of quality services to meet the needs of persons with disabilities involved in all areas of higher education. The Web site contains sections that focus on topics such as disability resources (best practices, civil rights laws, IDEA, universal design), students and parents, and special interest groups.

TRANSITION OF STUDENTS WITH DISABILITIES TO POSTSECONDARY EDUCATION: A GUIDE FOR HIGH SCHOOL EDUCATORS

http://www.ed.gov/about/offices/list/ocr/transitionguide.html

This guide was developed to provide high school educators with answers to questions students with disabilities may have as they get ready to move to the postsecondary education environment.

National Center on Secondary Education and Transition

http://www.ncset.org

This is a national resource for secondary transition including resources and effective practices. The National Center on Secondary Education and Transition (NCSET) coordinates national resources, offers technical assistance, and disseminates information related to secondary education and transition for youth with disabilities in order to create opportunities for youth to achieve successful futures. Its Web site contains information covering such topics as Self-Determination for Middle and High School Students, IEP and Transition Planning, Self-Determination for Postsecondary Students, Career Guidance and Exploration, and Postsecondary Education Supports and Accommodations.

Self-Advocacy Skills for College Students

http://www.ldonline.org/ld_indepth/postsecondary/ncld_selfadv.html

LD OnLine contains hundreds of expert-reviewed articles and resources for educators and parents about children and adults with learning disabilities and ADHD. Items of interest found within the College & College Prep section include articles on financial aid, college planning, and selecting a college; a Questions + Answers section addressing accommodations, student rights, modifications and assistive tech use on the SAT, among others; and information on transition, adults with LD, and accommodations and modifications.

Transition Coalition

http://www.transitioncoalition.org

The Transition Coalition Web site provides online information, support, and professional development on topics related to the transition from school to adult life for students with disabilities. The Publications section provides access to transition-related booklets and brochures. The Resources Section contains links to various Web sites addressing topics such as employment and vocational information, independent living, postsecondary education, and self-determination.

WNY COLLEGIATE CONSORTIUM AND DISABILITY ADVOCATES: THE COLLEGE ENVIRONMENT

http://www.ccdanet.org/ecp/collegesuccess/collegeenv

This portion of the organization's Web site highlights the differences between high school and college focusing on areas such as the academic environment, grading, knowledge acquisition, support, stress, and responsibility. It also provides links to resources to assist in preparation to attend college.

DIVISION ON CAREER DEVELOPMENT AND TRANSITION (DCDT)

http://www.dcdt.org

A division of the Council for Exceptional Children, this organization's focus is to promote efforts to improve the quality of and access to career/vocational and transition services, as well as increase the participation of education in career development and transition goals. The Web site contains several links to topics relevant to transition and planning. It also provides information regarding conferences and Web seminars.

EDUCATION QUEST FOUNDATION

http://www.educationquest.org

With a mission to improve access to higher education, the Education Quest Foundation provides a wealth of knowledge to be considered during the transition into college. The Web site offers free college planning and outreach services, as well as scholarship and grant information. The Students with Disabilities section addresses topics such as exploring career options, preparing for entrance exams, selecting a college, applying for admission and financial aid, and self-advocacy and your legal rights and responsibilities.

National Center for Learning Disabilities (NCLD)
http://www.ncld.org/content/view/1033/389
Working to ensure children, adolescents, and adults with learning disabilities have every opportunity to succeed in school, work, and life, the NCLD provides information to parents and students regarding many aspects of learning disabilities. The Teen Topics section provides relevant information needed to make smart decisions about school, relationships, and building the necessary skills for high school and future success.

Think College
http://www.thinkcollege.net
This Web site is about college and the things to consider before and while the student attends. There are many disability supports and services available that will help students learn and meet their goals. The For Families section of the Web site includes sample plans and schedules, as well as a Parent Checklist and a FAQ section. The For Students section contains entries on Things to Consider, Getting Started, Student Stories, Your Rights, and Paying for College.

Virginia College Quest
http://www.vacollegequest.org
This user-friendly "Guide to College Success for Students with disAbilities" provides a wealth information for students and parents. The site divides information into specific categories; each category contains useful links. The Paving the Way section contains links to articles addressing information students need to know when planning for a college education.

COLLEGEBOARD.COM: STUDENTS WITH DISABILITIES

http://professionals.collegeboard.com/testing/ssd

Designed to connect students to college success and future opportunities, CollegeBoard.com provides information regarding programs and services in college admissions, guidance, assessment, financial aid, enrollment, and teaching and learning. The site provides information and links to prepare students for the SAT, the PSAT/NMSQT, and the Advanced Placement Program (AP). The Web site is divided into three sections, For Students, For Parents and For Professionals. Each section has links that address areas such as Planning for College, College Board Tests, Finding a College, Applying for College and Paying for College.

ACCESS TRANSITION

http://www.ataccess.org/resources/fpic/transition.html

Found within The Alliance for Technology Access (a Web site connecting children and adults with disabilities to technology tools), Access Transition was created to assist in planning for what to do after high school. The information contained may help the student and parent know their rights and how to begin planning for the future. It is intended to provide a basic understanding of the process, student rights, and options. More detailed information on many topics may be found by following the links provided. These take you to other places in this site, other resources on the ATA site, and to other valuable Web sites. These links include access to information regarding education, employment, and living self-sufficiently. It also addresses the role of technology in transition. Presented in a question-and-answer format, the site guides the user through the various topics and provides relevant links.

NATIONAL TRANSITION NETWORK (NTN)

http://ici2.umn.edu/ntn/default.html

This Web site, formerly funded by the U.S. Department of Education, was created to provide support to states in the form of technical assistance and evaluation services. Its intent was to improve transition and School-to-Work policies, programs, and practices. Although no longer active, the site provides information regarding publications, workshops, and relevant information links.

TRANSITION MATTERS

http://www.transitionmatters.org

This site provides documents and links to information regarding postsecondary transition for students with Asperger's syndrome or high functioning autism. Links included address many areas such as Support and Advocacy, Postsecondary Education and Transition, and Independent Living and Employment.

THE COMMON APPLICATION

http://www.commonapp.org

The Web site is designed to make available services that support equity, access, and integrity in the college application process. It includes an online application used by many secondary schools to promote access by evaluating students using a holistic selection process. The application forms can be obtained from this site both online and in print.

SMART ABOUT COLLEGE

http://www.smartaboutcollege.org

Created by the Student Assistance Foundation, this site provides students and families with information necessary to prepare for postsecondary education. Topics covered in this site include how to's for getting into and paying for college. Also included in this site are free ACT and SAT practice tests.

EDUCATIONAL TESTING SERVICE

http://www.ets.org

Designed to advance the quality and equity in education, ETS provides assessments, research, and related services to students. Upon entering "accommodations" into the search bar, the user is presented with information regarding Testing Accommodations for Test Takers with Disabilities. This area addresses general information as well as accommodations for computer-based testing and paper-based testing. The site also provides a wide range of information on various testing topics including Tips for Test Takers and Resources for Test Takers.

BROWSEALOUD

http://www.browsealoud.com/page.asp?pg_id=80004

This program reads Web pages aloud for people who find it difficult to read online. Reading large amounts of text on screen can be difficult for those with literacy and visual impairments. It makes using the Internet easier for people who have low literacy and reading skills, English as a second language, dyslexia, and visual impairments.

NATIONAL SECONDARY TRANSITION TECHNICAL ASSISTANCE CENTER

http://www.nsttac.org

To make sure full implementation of IDEA occurs and to help students with disabilities and their families attain desired post-school outcomes, NSTTAC strives to support and improve transition planning, services, and outcomes for youth with disabilities. The Web site contains sections that address Legal Requirements, Evidence Based Practices, Postsecondary Resources, and Students and Families.

National Dissemination Center for Children with Disabilities (NICHCY)

http://www.nichcy.org

This site serves as a central source of information on legal issues, laws, and research-based educational practices for children with disabilities. The user is able to connect with research, access publications (in both English and Spanish), connect with others, have questions answered, and receive information tailored to specific needs.

U.S. Department of Education's Office for Civil Rights

http://www.ed.gov/about/offices/list/ocr/transition.html

This portion of the Web site contains a parent brief addressing the rights and responsibilities of students with disabilities. This site also contains other useful information such as How to File a Complaint and Topics A–Z.

Wrightslaw: IDEA 2004: Transition Services for Education, Work, and Independent Living

http://www.wrightslaw.com/idea/art/defs.transition.htm

Designed to provide up-to-date information about special education law and advocacy, this site contains articles, cases, newsletters, and resources on many topics of importance to parents. Sections found on this site include Training Programs, Publications, Advocacy Library, and Law Library. The site also contains information regarding transition services to education, work, or independent living.

The ACT

http://www.actstudent.org

This site provides preparation and registration information regarding the ACT Examination. A special link includes information for students with disabilities regarding accommodations to taking the test.

Start Here Go Further

https://studentaid2.ed.gov

This site provides information on financial aid services. Students can get federally supported information on applying college and applying for financial aid, as well as tools and resources prepared by the U.S. Department of Education. The site also allows students to create a personal financial aid and college search portfolio called MyFSA that tracks applications, compiles lists of student-preferred colleges, creates a profile for easy application fill-in, and provides calendars, career information, and financial aid resources.

The Career Key

http://www.careerkey.org

This site provides an online tool containing a career assessment that matches the student's personality with careers. It also includes information on how to judge career tests for credibility, career development, and educational options, and a career information blog.

How-To-Study: A Study Skills Resource Site

http://www.how-to-study.com

This site addresses the development of study skills. Links to articles include SAT Test Taking Tips, Essay Tests, Study Groups, and Study Habits, among many others. There also are sections that address college planning and college success. The site offers study-skills programs and guides in both English and Spanish.

Higher Education for People with Disabilities

http://www.txddc.state.tx.us/resources/publications/collegepdf.pdf

This resource guide provides numerous Web site links on a multitude of topics. Areas addressed include General College Information, Educational Alternatives, College Planning and Preparation for Students with Disabilities, Admissions Testing and Study Skills, as well as many other topics.

Preparing to Be Nerdy Where Nerdy Can Be Cool

http://www.professorsadvice.com

This Web site is a personal journey of a student with autism who attended college, but information also is provided that specifically addresses students on the autism spectrum and suggestions on how to succeed in college.

Great Schools: Involved Parents, Successful Kids

http://www.greatschools.net

Designed to inspire parents to participate in their student's education, this Web site contains information on many aspects of education. Under Education Topics, the user will find links addressing areas such as learning disabilities and college preparation.

Post ITT

http://www.postitt.org

Representing Postsecondary Innovative Transition Technology, this Web site provides information and resources to students considering college. It contains guidance activities, checklists, resources, and information to support the transition to postsecondary life.

College Grazing

http://www.collegegrazing.com

Designed to assist the student in finding a college that fits his or her needs, this site provides many interactive planning tools. It has a section addressing college visits called Before You Go, Key Questions to Ask that even includes an assessment chart. This site also has sections addressing planning tools and resources. The best feature of the site is the "Discovery Surveys, Munchings." The

13 "munchings" ask questions about the student's views regarding college. Results are presented in an easy-to-read chart or diagram.

References

Americans with Disabilities Act, 42 U.S.C. §§ 12102 et seq. (1990).

Bashir, A., Goldhammer, R., & Bigaj, S. (2000). Facilitating self-determination abilities in adults with LDD: Case study of a postsecondary student. *Topics in Language Disorders, 21*, 52–67.

Berger, S. L. (2006). *College planning for gifted students* (3rd ed.). Waco, TX: Prufrock Press.

Brinckerhoff, L., Shaw, S. F., & McGuire, J. M. (2001). Promoting access, accommodations, and independence for college students with learning disabilities. *Journal of Learning Disabilities, 25*, 417–429.

Chambers, C. R., Wehmeyer, M. L., Saito,Y., Lida, K. M., Lee, Y., & Singh, V. (2007). Self-determination: What do we know? Where do we go? *Exceptionality, 15*, 3–15.

College Board. (n.d.). *Guidelines: Basic requirements for disability documentation*. Retrieved October 7, 2008, from http://professionals. collegeboard.com/testing/ssd/application/guide/guidelines

Covey, S. R. (1989). *The 7 habits of highly effective people*. New York: Free Press.

Eckes, S., & Ochoa, T. (2005). Students with disabilities: Transitioning from high school to higher education. *American Secondary Education, 33*(3), 6–20.

ERIC Clearinghouse on Handicapped and Gifted Children. (1989). *College planning for students with learning disabilities* (ERIC Digest

466). Retrieved from http://www.ericdigests.org/pre-9213/college.htm

Field, S., Martin, J., Miller, R., Ward, M., & Wehmeyer, M. (1998). *A practical guide for teaching self-determination.* Reston, VA: Council for Exceptional Children.

Field, S., Sarver, M. D., & Shaw, S. F. (2003). Self-determination: A key to success in postsecondary education for students with learning disabilities. *Remedial and Special Education, 24,* 339–349.

Getzel, E. E., & Thoma, C. A. (2008). Experience of college students with disabilities and the importance of self-determination in higher education settings. *Career Development for Exceptional Individuals, 31,* 77–84.

Getzel, E. E., & Wehman, P. (2005). *Going to college: Expanding opportunities for people with disabilities.* Baltimore: Paul H. Brooks.

Gil, L. A. (2007). Bridging the transition gap from high school to college. *TEACHING Exceptional Children, 40*(2), 12–15.

HEATH Resource Center. (2003). *Creating options: A resource on financial aid for students with disabilities.* Washington, DC: George Washington University.

HEATH Resource Center. (2006). *Guidance and career counselors' toolkit: Advising high school students with disabilities on postsecondary options.* Washington, DC: George Washington University.

Hicks-Coolick, A., & Kurtz, P. D. (1997). Preparing students with learning disabilities for success in postsecondary education: Needs and services. *Social Work in Education, 19,* 31–42.

Individuals with Disabilities Education Improvement Act, PL 108-446, 118 Stat. 2647 (2004).

LDOnline. (2008). *College planning for students with learning disabilities.* Retrieved from http://www.LDOnline.org

Madaus, J. W. (2005). Navigating the college transition maze: A guide for students with learning disabilities. *TEACHING Exceptional Children, 37*(3), 32–37.

Madaus, J. W., & Shaw, S. F. (2006). The impact of the IDEA 2004 on transition to college for students with learning disabilities. *Learning Disabilities Research & Practice, 21,* 273–281.

Martin, J. E., Mithaug, D. E., Cox, P., Peterson, L. Y., Van Dycke, J. L., & Cash, M. E. (2003). Increasing self-determination: Teaching students to plan, work, evaluate, and adjust. *Exceptional Children, 69,* 431–447.

Martin, J. E., Van Dycke, J. L., Christensen, W. R., Greene, B. A., Gardner, J. E., & Lovett, D. L. (2006). Increasing student participation in IEP meetings: Establishing the self-directed IEP as an evidence-based practice. *Exceptional Children, 72,* 299–316.

Mason, C. Y., McGahee-Kovac, M., & Johnson, L. (2004). How to help students lead their IEP meetings. *TEACHING Exceptional Children, 36*(3), 18–25.

McCarthy, D. (2007). Teaching self-advocacy to students with disabilities. *About Campus, 12*(5), 10–16.

McGuire, J. M., & Shaw, S. F. (1987). A decision-making process for the college-bound learning disabled student: Matching learner, institution, and support program. *Learning Disability Quarterly, 10,* 106–111.

Murray, C., Goldstein, D. E., Nourse, S., & Edgar, E. (2000). The postsecondary school attendance and completion rates of high school graduates with learning disabilities. *Learning Disabilities Research & Practice, 15,* 119–127.

Nadeau, K. (2006). *Survival guide for college students with ADHD or LD.* (2nd ed.). Washington, DC: Magination Press.

National Center for Education Statistics. (2000). *Postsecondary students with disabilities: Enrollment, services, and persistence. Stats in Brief.* Washington, DC: U.S. Department of Education.

National Joint Committee on Learning Disabilities (NJCLD). (2007). The documentation disconnect for students with learning disabilities: Improving access to postsecondary disability services. *Learning Disability Quarterly, 30,* 265–274.

Newman, L. (2005). Postsecondary education participation of youth with disabilities. In M. Wagner, L. Newman, R. Cameto, N. Garza, & P. Levine (Eds.), *After high school: A first look at the postschool experiences of youth with disabilities. A report from the National Longitudinal Transition Study-2* (NLTS2, pp. 4-1–4-16). Menlo Park, CA: SRI International.

Palmer, A. (2006). *Realizing the college dream with Autism or Aspergers syndrome*. London: Jessica Kingsley Publishers.

Quinn, P. O., Ratey, N. A., & Maitland, T. L. (2000). *Coaching college students with AD/HD*. Washington, DC: Advantage Books.

Sandler, M. (2008). *College confidence with ADHD*. Naperville, IL: Sourcebooks.

Savukinas, R. (2003). *Community colleges and students with disabilities*. Retrieved from http://www.heath.gwu.edu/Templates/Newsletter/issue3/commcoll.htm

Scott, S. S. (1991). A change in legal status: An overlooked dimension in the transition to higher education. *Journal of Learning Disabilities, 24*, 459–466.

Section 504 of the Rehabilitation Act, 29 U.S.C. Section 706 et seq. (1973).

Shaw, S. (2008). *College opportunities for students with disabilities*. Retrieved from http://advocacyinstitute.org/projects/postsec_realistic_option.shtml

Shinn, M. R. (2007). Identifying students at risk, monitoring performance, and determining eligibility within response to intervention: Research on educational need and benefit from academic intervention. *School Psychology Review, 36*, 601–617.

Sitlington, P. L., & Clark, G. M. (2006). *Transition education and services for students with disabilities* (4th ed). Boston: Pearson.

Thompson, S. J., Morse, A. B., Sharpe, M., & Hall, S. (2005). *Accommodations manual: How to select, administer, and evaluate use of accommodations for instruction and assessment of students with disabilities* (2nd ed.). Retrieved from http://osepideasthatwork.org/tooklit/accommodations.asp

U.S. Department of Education, Office for Civil Rights (2007). *Students with disabilities preparing for postsecondary education: Know your rights and responsibilities*. Washington, DC: Author.

Van-Belle, J., Marks, S., Martin, R., & Chun, M. (2006). Voicing one's dreams: High school students with developmental disabilities learn about self-advocacy. *TEACHING Exceptional Children, 38*(4), 40–46.

Virginia Department of Education. (2003). *Virginia's college guide for students with disabilities.* Retrieved from http://www.doe.virginia.gov/VDOE/sped/transition/collegeGuide2003.pdf

Wehmeyer, M. L. (1996). Self-determination as an educational outcome: Why is it important to children, youth and adults with disabilities? In D. J. Sands & M. L. Wehmeyer (Eds.), *Self-determination across the lifespan: Independence and choice for people with disabilities* (pp. 1–14). Baltimore: Brookes.

Wehmeyer, M. L. (2002). *Self-determination and the education of students with disabilities.* Reston, VA: Council for Exceptional Children.

Wehmeyer, M. L., & Palmer, S. B. (2003). Adult outcomes for students with cognitive disabilities three years after high school: The impact of self-determination. *Education and Training in Developmental Disabilities, 38,* 131–144.

WNY Collegiate Consortium and Disability Advocates. (n.d.). *The college environment.* Retrieved October 13, 2008, from http://www.ccdanet.org/ecp/collegesuccess/collegeenv

ABOUT THE
AUTHORS

Cynthia G. Simpson, Ph.D., has more than 16 years of experience in the public and private sector as a preschool teacher, special education teacher, elementary teacher, educational diagnostician, associate professor of education, and administrator. She maintains an active role in the lives of children and young adults with exceptionalities as an educational consultant in the areas of assessment, inclusive practices, and transition planning. Her professional responsibilities include serving on the National Council for Accreditation of Teacher Education/National Association of Young Children Review Panel, as well as serving as a state advisor to the Texas Educational Diagnostician Association. Cynthia has many publications to her credit (books and articles) and is a featured speaker at the international, national, and state level. She currently is an associate professor and program coordinator for special education in the College of Education at Sam Houston State University. Cynthia has won several awards and received numerous recognitions for her work with individuals with disabilities, as well as her contributions to the field of special education.

Vicky G. Spencer, Ph.D., has served in the field of special education for more than 20 years as a special education teacher, educational consultant, and assistant professor. She also has worked for the Virginia Department of Education providing teacher training throughout the state focusing on a variety of academic areas dealing with students with special needs. Vicky continues to remain actively involved in the field as she collaborates with special education teachers to implement cognitive strategies within the inclusive classroom setting. Her current research interests include cognitive-strategy instruction for students with mild to moderate disabilities, autism, and transition planning. Vicky has presented findings from her research at state, national, and international conferences and published numerous articles that disseminate those findings. Vicky currently is an assistant professor and the Assistant Director of Operations at the Kellar Institute for Human disAbilities at George Mason University.